Secrets of Shaktipat and Kundalini Yoga

Volume – 3 (Q & A)

Colonel T Sreenivasulu

First published in India in 2020

Second edition: Jan 2023

Copyright © 2020 T Sreenivasulu

All rights reserved.

www.sahajananda-ashram.com

Dedication

I am inspired to dedicate this work to all the practitioners of kundalini yoga who have taken shaktipat initiation in the past and those who will be doing it in the future.

His Holiness Swami Sahajananda Tirtha, at the age of 85 in the year 2009, the venerable Guru of the author

Contents

Acknowledgements
Introduction
Foreword
Manifestation of kriyas
Shaktipat
Karma, creation, illusion, and scriptures
Samadhi, Anahata sound, dispassion, self-surrender, mantras, food habits, service to Guru, renunciation
General topics
Sex-related issues
Kundalini energy-related issues
Sadhan
Miscellaneous issues
Glossary
Ashrams of Shaktipat Order
Monks of the Order of Shaktipat
About the author

Acknowledgements

I am forever indebted to my venerable Guru, His Holiness Swami Sahajananda Tirtha, who made me a shaktipat Guru.

I am also deeply indebted to all the venerable Gurus of my lineage of the "Order of Shaktipat," whose collective wisdom has been the guiding light for me while venturing into some of the uncharted waters of this ocean of ancient knowledge.

I compliment all the practitioners who made the compilation of this book possible. If they had not persisted with their numerous doubts on the subject, I would not have possibly explored my mind so profoundly for throwing light on some of the lesser-known details regarding the subject.

I am grateful to Mr. Nagarajan Chidambaram, one of the practitioners who had painstakingly compiled the main bits of conversation between the other practitioners and me.

Introduction

The word shaktipat means the descent of energy. It is not an independent yoga system. It is simply an ancient yoga technique. However, it is the highest yoga technique or the mother of all yoga techniques known to mankind. In this, supreme cosmic power is used as the technique. The supreme cosmic power creates the cosmos at both individual and collective levels. Therefore, the efficient disintegration or destruction of the world can only be done by the cosmic power itself. Every human being is a miniature model of the cosmos, as per ancient Sanskrit texts. Therefore, whether at the macrocosm or microcosm level, the same cosmic power is involved in its creation, sustenance, and final disintegration. As a result, the only thing in the cosmos is this supreme cosmic power. It pervades the infinite cosmos. Even modern science admits this fact. The human bodies, with their flesh, blood, and bones, are also made out of this same cosmic power. However, the underlying substratum of this vast and infinite cosmos is unknown. We can call it the God, the

Almighty, the Brahman, the Atman, or the divinity. It is widely proclaimed in all ancient Sanskrit texts that the same substratum of the cosmos is also pervading everywhere infinitely. Therefore, whether it is cosmic power or the divine is the same as two sides of the same coin. From this perspective and as proclaimed in ancient Sanskrit texts, a human being is a miniature model of the cosmos; the same underlying substratum in the form of divinity pervades the human body too!

The self-realization for a human being is, therefore, becomes the only thing to be known or realized. Self-realization results in the realization of the cosmos too. That means if a drop of water in an ocean realizes its nature, it also knows the vast ocean. Therefore, there is no necessity for a human being to explore the vast and infinite depths of interstellar and intergalactic space.

The technique applied to achieve this realization in a human being is called shaktipat. The process which is affected by this technique is called yoga in general terms. The process terminates in self-realization, salvation, a merger with the universal spirit called God, etc.

Various yoga techniques have been developed since ancient times to achieve this grand aim of joining the individual soul with the universal soul. However, due to the gigantic nature of the task involved, it is impossible for a human being to affect this process on his or her own. All yoga or tantric techniques applied are geared solely to achieve a specific benchmark. That benchmark is to instigate the outbound cosmic power from its creative mode to retract itself. As a result, the same cosmic energy that had created the human being and their individual world starts to disintegrate by destroying the karma imprinted in their subconscious minds.

This benchmark is what is called the awakening of cosmic energy. However, there is nothing known as awakening as such in its classical sense of the meaning of the word. The all-powerful, all-knowing, and supreme cosmic power is always awakened as we understand the word. It is just the point at which it starts to retract itself from the creative and sustenance mode to the disintegrative or destructive mode is what we term as "awakening" for ease of our understanding of the subject.

The awakened cosmic energy in the terminology of human beings is called the awakening of kundalini energy. After creating a human being, this cosmic energy is supposed to lie in a dormant state at the base of the cerebral-spinal system in the human body. It is also considered to be continuously projecting or sustaining the illusion of "life" for a human being. This illusion is akin to a mirage in a desert that gives the optical illusion of water.

This benchmark is achieved for the practitioner in every path of the yoga or tantric system. As a result, there is nothing left for the yoga practitioner to do further. Whatever has to happen will happen without any effort from the yoga practitioner! The awakened cosmic energy does the process of disintegrating the world or destroying the individual karmas after it starts retracting or collapsing inwardly. Different names in different yoga systems call this energy. However, it is popularly known as kundalini energy.

Shaktipat is an exclusive yoga technique applied to awaken the kundalini energy. A little explanation is required here to understand the reason for this specialized yoga technique. The spiritual evolution of a spirit or the Atman of a human being can be broadly categorized into three stages. The first stage is before the awakening of kundalini energy! In this stage, all effort is put in by the yoga practitioner voluntarily, with egoism coloring all actions. All kinds of worship of God, yoga practices, tantric practices, etc., come under this category. However, the effort put in by the practitioner amounts to be very minute in nature. After the awakening of kundalini energy, the supreme cosmic power itself puts in the effort internally. As a result, the destruction of karma accumulated in a human being occurs rapidly and acceleratedly. This second stage terminates in thoughtlessness or samadhi, as it is called in Sanskrit texts. The third stage starts from here. However, there is no more yoga technique left for this stage. Hence, there is no known initiation into this absolute path. All ancient texts have remained silent after this. It is said in the texts that the final journey of the soul to achieve its merger with the universal soul or God occurs at the will of God.

Therefore, the technique of shaktipat deals with the second stage only. However, human beings must have practiced different yoga systems in their different past lives. As human being approaches a particular benchmark in their respective chosen paths for an awakening of cosmic energy, initiation is given by a Guru by using the technique of shaktipat. After shaktipat is done on a human being, it remains active forever until salvation is attained. That means shaktipat is carried forward to their afterlife. However, in every lifetime, it is mandatory to take formal shaktipat initiation under a Guru in a formal manner. When shaktipat is done on a person in whom the kundalini energy is already active by birth, it stabilizes at a safe level. In people in whom the kundalini energy has not been activated, it will get triggered for the first time, provided they have reached closer to the benchmark level, which I have explained above.

Therefore, shaktipat is meant in a way for some people only. It cannot be given to anyone. It may not work even if it is given. Destiny itself decides who is meant to receive shaktipat initiation. That means the karmas accumulated by the practitioners themselves in their past lives or current life will draw them towards the path of shaktipat. A Guru may suddenly appear out of nowhere and bless them with shaktipat deeksha. This is crucial to understand. Because of this, the technique is not very popular among mankind. That means people do not usually meet shaktipat Gurus in the first place. Probably due to the advancements in modern communication technology, people are hearing about it in recent times. However, the actual process of shaktipat initiation takes place or depends upon their past accumulated

Secrets of Shaktipat and Kundalini Yoga

karmas only. I wish to refrain from commenting upon many Gurus in recent times who may be offering to give shaktipat initiation for fees. Their authenticity cannot be taken for granted.

The author of this book is one of my disciples. I gave him a shaktipat initiation about 12 years ago. He has even written a book, "The Power Unknown to God," on his experiences during the awakening of kundalini energy. I have also given him the deekshadhikara, or the authorization to give shaktipat initiation to people at the beginning of 2019. He has been rendering his services to me tirelessly since then, giving shaktipat initiation to more than 200 people in less than a year.

Many people have numerous doubts regarding the subject, especially during the initial stages after taking shaktipat initiation. Guidance from a Guru is crucial during such stages. I am happy to see many of his practitioners asking numerous doubts about the subject. I am also pleased to see so many of them developing kriyas or reactions in their bodies and narrating them. Authentic literature concerning personal experiences available on such subjects is limited. Therefore, this book is priceless because it will add to the existing literature on the subject. Moreover, practitioners have explored the author's mind in such great depth by posing him with numerous questions covering almost all aspects of the issue. Hence, the title of the book "Secrets of Shaktipat and Kundalini Yoga" is quite apt.

May this book remain a beacon of knowledge to all kundalini yoga practitioners from all paths! May it contribute to the less-known subject concerning the practical intricacies of kundalini yoga practice! In recent times, there may be a massive volume of literature on kundalini yoga. But that is primarily theoretical in nature. The authentic knowledge which can be applied to the physical practice of the yoga system is limited. Therefore, this book will be of immense help to all yoga practitioners. Lastly, this book will also be an excellent resource for all shaktipat Gurus interacting with

Colonel T Sreenivasulu

their disciples.

- Swami Sahajananda Tirtha

Foreword

During the peak winter season of 2019, in January, I have been conferred with the honor of shaktipat deekshadhikara, or the authorization to give shaktipat initiation into kundalini yoga, by my venerable Guru, His Holiness Swami Sahajananda Tirtha. His Holiness is now 97 years old, living in the city of Vijayawada in the State of Andhra Pradesh in India. He has already stopped giving shaktipat initiation to people directly for a while now. I was initiated into kundalini yoga by shaktipat nearly 12 years ago by His Holiness in 2007. I have written my first book, "The Power Unknown to God," published in 2014, on my experiences during the awakening of kundalini energy. The book has been subsequently translated into 17 more world languages and published on several major platforms like Amazon.

When His Holiness first mentioned this a few years ago, I was completely reluctant to take on this sacred responsibility. I felt that it would be a distraction and a burden for me. Moreover, my Guru has already conferred the honor of giving shaktipat initiation to three of my fellow practitioners who have been on the job for some time now. Further, I always had this tendency to avoid taking on any kind of responsibility. Whenever I believed that a particular work could be handled by someone else, I simply avoided it quietly. Perhaps this is inbuilt into my blood. However, His Holiness has been insisting on it on a few occasions from time to time.

Before my Guru broached this topic of conferring this honor on me, I was already entrusted with the task of writing two more books on two different topics. One of the topics is the science of giving shaktipat initiation into kundalini yoga. This is in the wake of publishing my first book. I was surprised because writing such a book requires the skills of being a shaktipat Guru. Further, not much literature is available directly on the topic mentioned above. This means I would not have the benefit of referring to any books. This has given me the first indication of my Guru's future plans for me.

In 2019, I gave shaktipat initiation to more than 200 people from various backgrounds. This includes people from different religious, educational, professional, social, and ethnic backgrounds. The list also included some of my friends, for which I am grateful to the Almighty for allowing me to wipe off my karmic debt to them. The range of age for both men and women varied from 20 to 75 years. In some cases, teenagers as young as thirteen even approached me for shaktipat initiation into kundalini yoga. I had to flatly refuse on the pretext that they were still minors legally.

In some cases, parents themselves have brought their children for the initiation. Only in such instances in which parent involvement was there directly had I agreed to compromise with my strict age stipulation. Apart from this, I had to refuse to give shaktipat initiation to many more due to several reasons like suffering from major diseases, addiction to drugs, mental instability, mental retardation, vested interest in taking shaktipat initiation for materialistic gains, curiosity to gain supernatural powers, etc., However, I have never discriminated against anyone including those who are gender challenged or with different sexual orientation or with any kind of other issues like non-belief in God, etc.,

I was aware that many questions would be asked by

Secrets of Shaktipat and Kundalini Yoga

people, especially during the initial stages of practice. However, I had never expected to give shaktipat initiation to so many people in such a short period. I was also overwhelmed by both the volume and range of questions asked by the practitioners. In a way, practitioners have forced me to explore my mind within threadbare. Otherwise, I would have never explored myself so profoundly. Some of the questions asked by practitioners were rare from the point of their content. You don't find answers to such questions, usually anywhere among the existing literature on shaktipat and kundalini yoga. The idea of compiling my answers to questions never occurred to me initially. This was suggested by one of the practitioners later on. However, many questions and answers had already been missed by that time. Unfortunately, I don't remember those missed-out questions and answers now.

Later I had the idea of compiling the experiences also by different practitioners so that it would add to the existing literature on the science of shaktipat initiation into kundalini yoga.

Most of my answers to the questions are not new from the point of their content. They are consistent with the well-known phenomenon expounded by various Gurus of the shaktipat lineage. However, some of the questions have been answered with a slight modification so that the message can be understood by a wide range of people with different backgrounds. I have tried my best to keep the various religious and philosophical teachings out of the discussion. I have strictly adhered to the teachings of yoga texts.

This book is basically the compilation of various questions asked by the practitioners who have taken shaktipat initiation from me and their direct experiences in the aftermath of shaktipat initiation. A few questions asked by other practitioners who have not been initiated by me have also been included. Some of the questions asked by the practitioners have been deliberately not included since they were too personal, and this book would have gotten cluttered.

A massive quantity of literature is available worldwide in many languages pertaining to kundalini yoga practice. However, the available literature is mainly on awakening kundalini energy through various independent methods like Ashtanga yoga or Raja yoga. Literature available on shaktipat initiation into kundalini yoga is generally limited. Further, authentic personal experiences are rarely made public. Therefore, this book will benefit all the practitioners of kundalini yoga from various lineages. A general reader may find it informative as well as educative.

These are the secrets of brave practitioners who ventured into the much less-known waters of the ocean of knowledge.

May the supreme cosmic power in the form of awakened kundalini energy in their bodies guide them safely to cross this vast ocean of samsara or this worldly existence! May this shaktipat initiation into kundalini yoga free them all forever from the cycle of birth and death!

God bless you all.

- Author

Manifestation of kriyas

Kriyas related to mantra chanting

Question: A practitioner: Today, at the time of waking up, I had a strange experience. I observed that I was chanting the mantra, and I was confused. I was not aware whether I was doing sadhan or sleeping. I was continuously chanting mantras. It took 2-3 minutes for me to realize.

My response: There is nothing strange in that. It happens that way. The chanting of the mantra goes on subconsciously during the sleep state. It is a well-known phenomenon. I have also experienced it numerous times during my early days of sadhan.

Question: A practitioner: Today, when I sat for sadhan, I suddenly felt the urge to replace the mantra given by Guru Ji with; I am fire, I am water. Is there a specific reason for this?

My response: It's kriya only because you must have done Japa of those mantras in your past lives. Those karmas are now being cleaned up.

Question: A practitioner: I have just sat for 1 hour and had the same tones in my ear. So, I kept silent to listen to these tones. Then, the silence went on for around 10 minutes; I observed the tones and saw beautiful scenery. Next time shall

I keep repeating the mantra when these tones arise, or is it okay to tune in with them, like I did today? Jerks and vibrations were also happening intensely in different parts of my body.

My response: The mantra should stop naturally. That means your mind should get diverted from the mantra chanting naturally and without you stopping it. That is the thumb rule. After the mantra stops, then you, please keep watching the kriyas like a mute spectator. If you remember later that mantra chanting is not taking place, then let it be so. You don't have to go back to mantra chanting again. That is the thumb rule.

Kriyas related to crying

Question: A practitioner: For the past few days, on some occasions, I feel like crying, and many a time, my eyes have tears almost by seeing a movie or listening to a song. This had never happened before. I am not a guy to cry over silly things. I am also not able to sit in sadhan for a longer time. Why Guru Ji?

My response: Excellent; kriyas pertaining to the sheath of mind or Manomaya Kosha are also happening for you regularly now. They may continue over a prolonged period. You just need to remain in a state of witness whenever they manifest. Please never try to resist them, however negative they might appear to be.

About your inability to sit for a longer duration, please don't worry about it at this stage. Recently only your aggressive kriyas have subsided. Let the sadhan take its course. Let it stabilize first. On your part, just surrender yourself completely to the divinity. That is all you need to do. Later, you will be able to do sadhan for a longer duration. Please have patience and perseverance. It is a lifelong journey. No need to rush through the sadhan. It is more applicable to you because you have recently undergone very violent kriyas. You had to stop your sadhan also for a few days.

Secrets of Shaktipat and Kundalini Yoga

Question: Same practitioner: On the evening of initiation, I, too, cried for 10 minutes after listening to a Hindustani classical. I did not hear the singer before nor understood the language. Neither have I been in the habit of crying for the last 30 years.

My response: After Shaktipat initiation, the subconscious mind is subjected to a churning effect. As a result, all sorts of emotions and various sensual impressions try to rush out. Please don't try to stop the outburst of emotions in any way. It is happening for your own good. It is meant to clean off your karma related to that particular emotion.

Violent kriyas

Question: A practitioner: After receiving Shaktipat initiation from you this morning at 8:00 AM, I sat for sadhan for 85 minutes. Just 15 minutes into sadhan, I felt heaviness in my head. My heartbeat increased, and my entire body became heavy as if my body was ballooning out and about to explode.

Meditation had become very difficult, but I did not open my eyes.

Gradually, I became normal. After about half an hour, again for 15 to 20 seconds, I went through an experience where it seemed someone had taken possession of my body. The experience was accompanied by a bit of pain. This is an experience in my life that I can never forget.

My response: Excellent, kriyas have started for you full-blown on the day of Shaktipat deeksha itself. However, please don't worry about the violent kriyas. It is happening for your own good. Nothing will happen to you. You told me that you tried to stop the sadhan by trying to remember your Guru at that time. Please don't try to stop the kriyas as far as possible unless they become too uncomfortable. I am very happy for you. This is the beginning of your spiritual journey. Lastly, please be brave but exercise complete self-surrender to God.

Colonel T Sreenivasulu

Question: A practitioner: I sat in sadhan for 1 hour. I feel pain in the whole neck, especially the thyroid gland. I sense full vibrations in the forehead and chest beating with full force, which is quite uncomfortable.

My response: Okay, very nice. Please take care of the pain. Please follow the procedure I told you if you feel that kriyas are happening too violently. Just stop the sadhan and divert your mind to any materialistic thoughts.

Question: A practitioner: I have a lot of kriyas happening in my head. It is unbearable; I am unable to open my eyes. I have stopped doing sadhan for the past three days, yet kriyas are happening. The mantra chanting is happening in my mind, and my eyes automatically close with concentration at the point between the eyebrows.

My response: Okay, please don't worry about it. Please divert your mind to your daily routine. Watch TV, read a newspaper, listen to some songs, go shopping, speak to your friends or relatives, and don't think about anything on spiritual matters.

Question: A practitioner: Sharing my last night experiences in sadhan. As soon as I closed my eyes, there appeared brightness. As the light was getting brighter and brighter, it was becoming hard for me to offer my prostrations to the Guru Parampara. I experienced very heavy vibrations all over my body. Some currents were experienced on my neck, shoulders, wrists, and toes. I heard some loud noise as if something had struck the roof. I heard a sound like that of firecrackers in a sequence inside my room. I experienced a couple of times a sudden surge of energy from my Heart to the whole body. As I was prostrating before our lineage of Gurus, I felt Shivom Thirth Ji smiling at me. But my headache is not leaving me, despite taking medicines. Especially, I noticed it to be more intense on or near the full moon and new moon days. Please guide.

My response: Appearance of brightness is a very good kriya. I am very happy for you. Please don't worry about the pain in the head. It must have been some sort of heaviness you must be experiencing. That is kriya only. However, if it becomes unbearable, please immediately take a break from sadhan. There is nothing wrong with stopping the sadhan temporarily for a regular practitioner like you. Sadhan can be resumed again after you feel better.

Question: A practitioner: My body was rotating initially during meditation. After my body rotations ended, I felt a triangle-like spin at the bottom. After this kind of rotation, I felt like concentrating my body and mind on one particular point. I became utterly still after this. My head began to rotate differently, and finally, my tongue came out. My tongue then started to twist and began to move upwards. I felt pain and stopped the sadhan. After 5 minutes, I was like a mad person. I wanted to throw and destroy everything. It continued for one hour. Now I am alright.

My response: Excellent, they are all kriyas only. Nothing to worry about them. Whenever kriyas happen violently, please stop doing sadhan immediately and divert your mind to materialistic things. Focus your mind on worldly activities. Go for a walk or shopping or watch TV, etc. Focus your mind on anything other than spiritual subjects. Then automatically, kriyas will subside. After taking a break for one or two days, you can resume your sadhan.

Question: A practitioner: I did my 50 minutes of meditation. Sensations in the spine start immediately and rise to the top of my head. It was like a wifi connection. I could feel 3 bars higher above my head, and it continued like waves from Muladhara and high above my head. My third eye and face felt as if I had rubbed ice. The Ajna chakra is perpetually like as if iced.

Other than that, I could feel a lot of energy in my hands and a bit of burning in my body and stomach. I felt heat in

Muladhara. I realized one thing; every time I gave gratitude to the Gurus, my energy instantly started to rise. As for the posture, I felt when my back was straight and my shoulders were not stiff, which unknowingly happened, and when I released the stiffness, the energy flow was great.

My response: I am glad that your sadhan time is increasing. It is good to increase it to around an hour or more. You are experiencing a lot of kriyas which is very good for your progress. Surrendering to Guru is the key. Those who don't understand it in the true sense will have delayed progress. The initial posture should be straight but not very stiff. Gradually the energy may change your posture also. Once the kriyas start, it is better not to interfere with anything, even the posture. Let the energy work its way in the manner it wants to.

Question: A practitioner: Pranam Guru Ji, for the past 3-4 days, I have had severe pain in my Ajna Chakra, the center of the eyebrows. I have pain in my forehead too. Because of this, I am not able to do my sadhan. Please suggest why it is happening?

My response: Actually, it is kriya only. Whenever Ajna Chakra or the third eye region gets activated, it is known to be a little uncomfortable. You need to just endure it. If it becomes uncomfortable, you can stop the sadhan for a day or two. Otherwise, no need to worry about it.

Question: A practitioner: I was very sick yesterday. So, I did not sit for meditation. But in the evening, when I was just listening to a song on the headphone, I felt a tingle in the root chakra. My attention turned to that place. Slowly, the pain began to spread to the chakra of the Manipura chakra. After a while, something went up from the Muladhara Chakra to the Manipura chakra. It was like that for 20 minutes. Then it went up again and reached the chest. It was then that I started to feel something swell in my throat. It has been a while. I talked to you about it. You told me to take it as + ve. Now I am happy.

I found a kundalini page on Facebook. The guy said he knows you. When people mention the movement of energy within them, they describe that you can only feel energy flowing when you have blocks. When there are no blocks, you won't feel anything again. Is this true? I have a flowing feeling which is spiral-like from bottom to top. Then I have the bolting energy all over. I have a revolving head sometimes, and now random movements happen all over. Still, they seem very busy when I meditate.

My response: It is like this. It depends upon what people mean by blockages. Otherwise, kundalini energy is so subtle that there is nothing known as a blockage. Do you feel the x-rays entering your body when you get your x-ray done in a laboratory? How can anyone feel kundalini energy if you can't feel anything about such physical energy? It is subtler than the human intellect. It is the primordial form of power. Then how can anyone feel it?

Only its impact is felt when it is burning down karma. That impact is what we call kriya. That impact can be on your intellect, mind, internal body systems, the gross body, and external daily routine. Therefore, please don't get carried away by all such limited talk. People who talk like that may be partially true, but that is not the whole story.

For example, you know that the entire cerebrospinal system is integrated with the whole body. Their impact is felt when karmas are cleaned up by the awakened kundalini energy. Once the karma is cleared, their impact becomes subtler and subtler. That is why we say that kriyas die down ultimately. In this sense, if people want to use the terminology of blockage to represent a kriya manifestation, then it is up to them. But it is not a blockage in the classical sense.

Since the cerebrospinal system is linked with your subconscious mind, where karmas are accumulated, those karmas act as a blockage, so energy flow is felt. Otherwise, it is the cleaning of karmas that are experienced and not if any blockage is there. Literature such as this is confusing everyone and wasting time and effort. I suggest you, please avoid going anywhere near such literature.

Question: A practitioner: Sharing my experiences in yesterday's sadhan. It lasted for almost 3 hrs and 40 minutes. I felt pains and currents on my stomach, left ribs, navel, sudden movements, and jerks on my hand and face. Something started moving at the back of my spine near the Root Chakra.

I experienced sudden sweating, hot and cold feelings and some kind of pressure felt all over my body. Felt very heavy in my eyes and head all throughout my sadhan. Even after the sadhan, there were currents on the back of my shoulder and right leg, navel, and stomach region. I was feeling some kind of sore throat because of excessive activity in the throat Chakra. After yesterday's sadhan, it all became normal.

My response: Okay, very nice. Heaviness in the head is a kriya only. It is experienced whenever there is strong karma encountered by the awakened kundalini energy. It is a very common kriya. Please don't worry about it, and please continue your practice the same way.

Disruption of sleeping cycles

Question: A practitioner: I have woken up in the middle of my sleep 2-3 times for some days now. Are these kriyas?

My response: Yes, please. They are kriyas only. Disturbance in sleeping cycles is a known phenomenon after Shaktipat deeksha. But it is happening for your own good. We don't know how and why. But please endure it since it is happening to clean your karma only.

Question: A practitioner: For the last 5 days, in the night, I am not able to sleep due to restless legs. Legs become heavy and spontaneously change into different positions, but this happens continuously throughout the night. When will my sleeping pattern become normal again?

My response: Okay, disruption of the sleeping cycle is a well-known phenomenon after Shaktipat initiation. You need to endure this, please. If you continue with your sadhan regularly, you will overcome this problem in due course. However, it can't be predicted regarding the timeline, and it will obviously depend on your sadhan. There is no need to worry about it. Once a practitioner is on the yoga path, these issues should be minor, and one needs to endure them patiently.

Question: A practitioner: My sleeping time has been reduced. Yesterday night I slept at 3:00 AM. While sleeping, kriyas started. First, at the bottom of the spine, energy rotation was experienced. After some time, it moved toward the center of the spine and began to rotate. First, it spun towards the four edges, and after some time, it concentrated towards a center point.

My response: Okay, very nice. I am very happy for you. Then, please don't do any sadhan for a few days. Because kriyas are happening for you aggressively. Sadhan is, as such, not required. If kriyas become more violent, please divert your mind to normal worldly subjects. Please don't think about anything about spirituality. Just don't worry about it.

Heaviness in head

Question: A practitioner: In today's sadhan, for the initial 20 minutes, everything was going well, but after some time, I did not understand my head became very heavy and stressed. I concluded my sadhan and got up.

My response: Heaviness inside the head or cerebral region is a routine kriya. It happens whenever the awakened kundalini energy faces strong karma opposing it. As a result of the internal fight between the awakened kundalini and the opposing karma, the effect is experienced as heaviness inside the head. There is nothing to worry about it; it is happening for your own good. You need to just endure it. However, you can stop sadhan temporarily for the day if it is too uncomfortable.

Question: A practitioner: I have a lot of heaviness near my neck and back. Sometimes there is a lot of spinning near the third eye. I usually have a lot of issues around the head, along with the vibrations in my spine. I have many dreams, and sometimes they feel as if they are real. It has been a while since I am not active in the group, but I am doing sadhan, and this is what is happening to me these days.

My response: Okay, excellent. That means you are undergoing cerebral kriyas nowadays. They happen that way only. Little uncomfortable sometimes! But nothing to worry about it at all! These kriyas are experienced when the awakened kundalini faces some opposing solid karma.

Question: A practitioner: After my sadhan, when the divine energy is in my head or hand, I feel heaviness there. If the energy is in my head, I feel intoxicated. Guru Ji! what should I do? Should I restart my sadhan? The previous day after the sadhan, I felt heaviness in my hand. I continued my sadhan for 3 hours, but still, the heaviness was there.

My response: Okay. Very nice. I am pleased to see your progress. Kriyas are happening for you as such regularly without even doing sadhan. Sometimes you are experiencing kriyas aggressively also. Therefore, the important thing here is your sadhan management. Please stop the sadhan temporarily if kriyas are happening aggressively. Otherwise, please restart it slowly. That is how you need to manage it. Hence There is nothing known as to when to restart sadhan formally. It depends on how comfortable you are.

Fear related kriyas

Question: A practitioner: I feel fear when I do sadhan in the evening. I also feel that someone is with me. So, I can't complete sadhan, but in the morning, it is okay. How will I overcome the fear?

My response: It is kriya only. There is nothing to be afraid of at all. You should not stop your sadhan during such a time. Please be brave. Your karmas related to fear were getting cleaned. If you become afraid and stop your sadhan, those karmas will not get cleaned. Many practitioners in our group also experienced the same type of kriya. Some ladies have even experienced it as if they were touched by someone. But they are all kriyas only. I hope you keep your house or room locked inside while doing sadhan. Then where is the problem? You need to undergo the emotion of fear. That is important. I hope you understand it.

Question: A practitioner: I did experience some sensation. But I cannot know precisely why I felt a strong warm sensation in my back all the way to the head; and in my body in front side. I was overwhelmed with a feeling similar to fear.

A black spot appeared in front of the head (eyes closed). At that moment, I intensified chanting your name and picture as well as other Gurus, and then everything calmed down! At the exact moment, I experienced this, across the building where I live, some neighbor opened a window. That sound felt loud because my window was open; I live on the 5th floor. Yes, my mind produced many distractive thoughts, but I kept chanting names and thinking of Gurus' pictures.

My response: Okay, very nice. It seems kriyas are showing signs of manifestation. But let's observe more of them over the coming days. Please do not try to remember the Guru deliberately when intense kriyas are manifesting. Then obviously, kriyas will calm down. One is not supposed to do that. One needs to endure the kriyas as much as possible and remain in a state of witness. That means observing them, undergoing the emotion, or going with the flow.

Colonel T Sreenivasulu

Question: A practitioner: During my practice this evening, I had tingling sensations all over my face, especially my nose. Every time I felt I was accessing kriyas faster. A few thoughts crop up on the way, but I finally could focus. Then, the layers began to dissolve. They were taken away from my energy field; fear, limitation, and others I can't express in words. I felt them dissolve away. It also felt as if something was being removed from my heart center. My breath slowed so much that I thought I could forget to breathe. I also felt my heartbeat, and I have been feeling it in previous practices. So much gratitude comes to my heart.

How do I know when I should be coming back? Today, again, I felt a bit of fear as I got more profound, but I kept trying to fully surrender and trust. I became much more aware throughout my day and empowered in my presence.

My response: Please don't worry about when to stop the meditation. It will happen on its own. Just let it be that way. Please remember that kriyas are happening for you involuntarily without any effort from your side. The same phenomenon is possible the other way too. But kriyas as such may continue because they go on round the clock. But your practice session will end forcibly due to pain in your legs or other disturbances. Hence, no need to think about it at all.

Question: A practitioner: I feel fearful to continue with the sadhan. At that moment, I fully become like a kali mata. If it happens again, what should I do? Will it happen again? Usually, the continuity of kriya happens to me. I worshiped and prayed to kali mata. My kula devi is kali mata. Does this have any relation with that experience? While doing sadhan, I saw a triangle with a spot in its center.

My response: There is no need to worry at all. Everything is happening for your own good. It is happening to clean your karma only. The worship of kali, which you did previously, is also accumulated in your subconscious mind as karma. Those karmas are also required to get cleaned up. Everything is happening because of your past puja and sadhan only. Those karmas are also needed to be cleaned for your good. Then, only your mind will start entering samadhi. Otherwise, those karmas will stop your spiritual growth.

Please understand that you are now on the path of yoga. Yoga is different from religious practice. Because of your good karma, like worship of Kali, etc., only you have reached this stage. Shaktipat is the highest yoga technique known to mankind. There is no need to worry. Nothing adverse will happen to you. You need to be brave and self-surrender yourself to the divinity or Guru. If kriyas happen again, please use the same technique I told you about.

Just stop your sadhan temporarily and divert your mind to materialistic things or worldly activities. Kriyas will automatically subside. After resting for a day or two, you can start again! You are not the first person experiencing these kinds of violent kriyas. Other sadhaks also experienced such kriyas. They have also done the same thing. Therefore, please don't worry. Trust your Guru and the ancient yoga system.

Question: A practitioner: I want to explain a panic situation that repeated on the night of our initiation and yesterday. I would like to mention it in detail. On the night of Shaktipat, around 8 O'clock, I found difficulty swallowing and breathing. My body temperature fell sharply, and I was about to faint. In healing terminology, it was a psychic attack due to some elementals.

So, it was removed and followed by thorough healing. I was normal. The same issue occurred yesterday at the same time, also with similar symptoms. After recovery, it subsided. That is why I want to explain this in detail. This was the first time in my life this much trauma had occurred. The situation was somewhat out of control. Even though I had psychic attacks previously, they hadn't created this much havoc. Could you put some light on this?

My response: They are kriyas only. You are trying to compare it with other forms of healing etc. After Shaktipat deeksha, all your karmas start getting neutralized. Obviously, all such aggressive kriyas may start happening. You need to exercise self-surrender to the Guru and remain calm, observing them as witnesses.

If kriyas become aggressive, you should stop doing sadhan immediately and divert your mind away from all spiritual things. But you need to stop comparing Shaktipat with various other things. Shaktipat happens to be a higher yoga technique. It is meant to neutralize all your karma, whether good or bad. Good karmas, like worshipping gods and goddesses, chanting mantras, etc., will also get burned down.

Question: A practitioner: I was not sure if I was sleeping. I had experienced energy trying to dominate me. I had to face it then it disappeared. I had some terrific experiences twice today. Another was in the afternoon, and I saw a lizard on my hand. I could not move my body. I couldn't even shout. Finally awoke with a really strange shout; others were shocked hearing me cry. I believe this was the dream, but I am doubtful about the earlier one.

My response: The first one must have been the Tandra state, between the dream and waking states! That must be kriya. The second one is a strange dream that usually happens after Shaktipat initiation. But there is nothing to worry about them at all. They are happening for your own good, to clean up your karma. Many such strange experiences might be there in the future, also. I am pleased to see your progress. Just continue with your sadhan the same way. Be brave.

Speaking in unknown languages

Question: A practitioner: My practice today. I could focus so much on my Guru and chant my mantra. I felt connected in my heart center and did not need to judge my thoughts or my kriyas. I felt excited to share this with you, but something told me the emotion came from my ego. So, I immediately returned to the actual observing space. I felt so much peace; I also felt like not even my body defined everything I was. Then, I didn't feel attached to my body somehow.

Then, some words in a different language came to mind, and I could not help but speak these languages, words. When I spoke the word, I felt who I truly was. It is hard to describe with words, but I connected with something that felt very true and resonated with my being. I also had a flashback of when I was a kid. I would speak in a different language when I got deep in prayer. But then again, this is just an experience in the past.

My response: Very nice. They are kriyas only. Cleaning of your karma accumulated in the past is going on. Speaking an unknown language is a well-known phenomenon after Shaktipat. I am very happy to see your progress. Please continue with it the same way. The flashbacks were your past karmas accumulated in one of your previous lives. You must have had a solid connection with some language. Those sensual impressions were probably showing up. This usually happens. Therefore, you would have experienced them as a child, although you have not taken any Shaktipat initiation. Sometimes these things are experienced during the dream state as well.

Resisting kriyas during sadhan

Question: A practitioner: I wanted to try something different this morning as my practice is getting capped at under 100 minutes. Usually, I practice at 5:30 am but woke up at 4:30 am. I usually take water, but I gave that a miss. The energies were different right away. Kriyas started as I started my prayers to the "Monks of the Shaktipat Order." I could see the faces again of people I did not recognize. People with half faces presented themselves to me and tried to engage with me, winking and smiling at me.

Then I felt an electric shock on my head around the perimeter of my skull and another lesser one in my

Muladhara area. Next, a woman was proposing to me for sex. I initially said yes and then declined to hold my integrity. Reached 100 minutes of sadhan comfortably but felt tired afterward. Then lay on the ground, practiced there for a while, and drifted to sleep. I woke up feeling very refreshed. I also had electric sensations across the top of my left shoulder and spine.

My response: As I said earlier on several occasions, just remember not to stop or resist the kriyas during sadhan, however unethical or unpleasant or disgusting, or sinful they may be. Just remain a silent spectator and observe the kriyas. That is the bottom line. That is the principle of sadhan. Otherwise, the accumulated karma or sensual impressions in your subconscious mind will not get cleaned up. Lastly, please remember that whatever kriyas are happening is for your own good. Just exercise complete self-surrender and go with the flow of kriyas so that your accumulated karmas are washed away rapidly.

Aggressive kriyas

Question: A practitioner: Kriyas are happening from my Ajna Chakra to my Sahasrara Chakra. As a result, my eyes get closed. My mind dwells on the Ajna Chakra, even watching TV or interacting with my friends. Kriyas are very strong, and the energy is pulling towards the Sahasrara Chakra. Particularly today, the kriya is intense.

My response: Please don't worry. Try to divert your mind away from all kinds of spiritual thoughts. Please focus on routine life issues. Watch TV or read newspapers, etc. Just do anything else other than spiritual-related things. Kriyas will subside.

Question: A practitioner: I have been having kriyas since night. Ever since I slept. I felt vibrations in my heart and head, but I slept. Later at 1:00 or 2:00 AM, I felt strong vibrations in my heart and head. It was powerful, and some energy wanted me to remove the clothes.

Secrets of Shaktipat and Kundalini Yoga

I did so. I then rubbed my hands over my body and felt the energy getting released. The process was intense, and I was in bed. I wanted to get up, but the vibrations were still there, and somehow, I slept for an hour. Then, I started my sadhan after I woke up. Energies in my head, lips, nose, and eyes were apparent.

Once again, the energies were too high, and I loosened my clothes finally and surrendered to the energies. I felt better and more connected after doing so. And later, when I got up from my sadhan and closed my eyes to see the light in my third eye, I saw a coiled green snake. Do the snake, and these kriyas indicate something? Please guide.

Later on, I could feel a kissing sensation on my lips. While during my regular puja, the kriyas repeated. I was moving like a pendulum front to back. As my puja ended, the movement stopped. Emotions are a part of life, and when we connect with anyone. They are natural; emotions vary with time, and the energies will always be there.

My response: Kriyas are happening for you now, full-blown. There is nothing to worry about it at all. Obviously, energy movement will be experienced by you in every nook and corner of your body. But why were you trying to stop the kriyas by rubbing your body with your hands? You should avoid doing that. They were happening for your own good. If it is only energy flow, you shouldn't scratch or rub or try to feel it with your hand, etc. Otherwise, kriyas might stop manifesting.

Removing clothes or loosening clothes is perfectly normal. You can do that. The vision of the coiled snake is auspicious only. Kriyas also manifest in the form of emotions since they are part of life, as you said. Please don't try to resist them during sadhan, whether they are pleasant or unpleasant. Please, continue with your sadhan the same way regularly. That is all you need to do.

Colonel T Sreenivasulu

Question: A practitioner: Today, the external kriyas were mild again – a few times came to the nodding of the head, pendulum movement of the body, turning the head left and right, small circles made with the head. Between movements, there were long periods of stillness and deep weightlessness.

The whole body felt electrified – many small currents were appearing in the entire body. The crown chakra had the electrical current throughout the whole practice as well. There was also the big, spiral wave of energy going from the Muladhara all the way up to the crown. There was also a crawling sensation on my whole body, including my forehead, and an expansive wave of small currents traveling up from the bottom of my back.

Again, the third eye was pulsating as if something was pushing it from the inside. At the same time, there was a crawling sensation felt from the outside. The pulsating push was felt the whole time.

After some time, a strange pain appeared – first just in the Anahata Chakra. It was like dull, hollow pain, as if there was a "ball of pain" inside of my chest. It lasted for maybe 5 minutes. Then the pain appeared again but this time in Muladhara, and stayed for some time there. Then it traveled again – I felt it also in Svadhisthana, Manipura, Anahata, Visuddha, and Ajna. It was the strongest in the Muladhara and in Anahata Chakra.

After I finished practice, it stopped immediately. I practiced for 1 hour and 52 minutes, and again – it felt speedy.

I have also noticed a change in my everyday life - the fears, aggregation, restlessness, and pain - everything is gone! I am blissful, happy, and balanced. I even lost interest in some activities that I used to do before - I am more focused now.

My response: Excellent. You are experiencing the kriyas full-blown. There is nothing else to be done other than continuing your sadhan. Of course, please keep your mind focused on your Guru always. Otherwise, the sense of I'ness or a feeling of pride starts developing. You should be in a state of a witness or remain a mute spectator as the kriyas unfold. Otherwise, kriyas themselves become freshly accumulated as karmas in the subconscious mind.

Question: A practitioner: I noticed that my digestive system gets erratic whenever I cross the 5-hr mark in my Sadhan. A couple of days before, it was overactive. Now I am Okay. Also, I am disturbed during Sadhan these days. It was never the case before. Yesterday night after 4 hrs in Sadhan:

Apart from mild Kriyas and visions of radiance, I have many thoughts these days. In fact, I never had the issue of thoughts coming up in my Sadhan. Also, there was turmoil inside me in every part of my life during the Sadhan time.

A debate occurs about life, Illusion, and Reality going on inside me. Questions like: What difference does it make if I die now or later in life if everything is an Illusion? If it is now, I will only realize earlier that it is all illusion and done with it. If it is later, I will realize after that many years and be done with it.

Ultimately, it is all illusion, either now or later. What, then, is the reality? And how do we know about it if everything is an illusion?

Also, the enormous path of life I underwent was just to remain in this illusion. Is it really worth it? I seem to be lost everywhere.

My response: Excellent. I am very happy for you. They are all kriyas only. There is nothing to worry about it at all. Similarly, there is no guidance required for you either. Everything is happening for you properly. Thoughts are meant to arise, including the internal discussion kind of thing which you experience. Just let it go on. Please don't resist the thoughts. There is nothing strange about it at all. Slowly and steadily, your mind and your life will start undergoing rapid transformation.

Question: A practitioner: Sharing my experiences in sadhan. I experienced that my whole room was full of bright light when I closed my eyes. As if I am sitting in broad daylight. My entire focus was on the brightness all through my sadhan. My body felt very light. I lost the sensation of my breathing. There were occasional pains and pressures on my ears, stomach, navel, and ribs, and itching on my palms. There were hot and cold flashes with sudden sweating and cold sensations. After my sadhan, as I opened my eyes, I got scared as it was complete darkness outside. It was 00:40 AM local time here. The whole sadhan lasted for about 3 hrs and 40 minutes.

My response: That is a very good kriya. It is a sign of excellent progress on the path of yoga. I am delighted to see your progress. Please continue with your practice the same way. We will observe more of it in the coming days.

Question: A practitioner: Sharing my last night experiences during sadhan. I experienced kriyas of bending for nearly 30 minutes. After that, I had visions of bright light. Sometimes the light was becoming really bright. I experienced lots of kriyas in my stomach area! I have a severe cluster headache on the right side of my head and felt heavy pressure in my right ear. My head feels unusually heavy. In between felt very cold. The whole time I felt very restless. I was experiencing a lot of kriyas in my digestive system! I feel it is overactive. Unusual bowel movements were experienced for the whole day. In the mid-afternoon, I had a severe cluster headache. I took a nap at 6:00 pm. My head feels shaky. After 3.5 hrs, I stopped my sadhan. Even today, I have persistent headaches and uneasiness.

My response: Okay. Please take a break for a day or two. It seems kriyas are becoming a little aggressive. Let them subside a little. Please divert your mind to normal worldly activities. Later you can resume your sadhan once again. Please remember that sadhan is not supposed to be done forcefully in our path.

Question: A practitioner: Duration- 5 hrs. Lots of emotions surfaced in the beginning. The vision of brightness on my Third Eye Chakra remained throughout my Sadhan. I also experienced Physical Kriyas of bending, swinging, body rotations, and neck rotations. At one point, I felt something moving down from my neck to the Heart Chakra along the spine.

My response: Excellent. Kriyas are manifesting for you. Kundalini Shakti is activated and clearing your past accumulated karmas. You do not need to worry about anything. A sadhak experiences such events after the activation of the kundalini. Keep doing sadhan the same way. Have firm faith in your Guru.

Question: A practitioner: In the car on the way to work – electric current on the top of the head, wrists, forehead, arms, and so on.

EVENING

I felt mild external kriyas – head nodding, head pulling, and pendulum movement of the body. I felt electric currents on the top of the head, on the back of the head, and on the forehead. I practiced for 30 minutes only due to immense tiredness.

Next day:

Throughout the day, I felt recurring electric currents on the top of my head and wrists, and my body was a little electrified.

EVENING

Kriyas started immediately when I closed my eyes. There were repeating movements: pendulum movement of the body, circles of the body beginning in the Muladhara, bending to the left and right with the head. The most prominent were head movements – nodding, left to right, and small and bigger circles. Also, an infinity pattern drew my head in the air. All those mild kriyas were repeating themselves through ¾ of the sadhan.

The main kriya was, again – the electric current. First appeared on the top of the head, then more in the front of the head. The body felt electrified. Small currents were appearing all over the body. The wrists were prominent again. A solid electric current on the back in the lowest region was moving a little bit up along the spine, creating almost a burning sensation.

Many popping/cracking/explosive sounds in the head, with small explosions accompanying it, all over the head. Rattle sound and concentrated stream of those small explosions – felt inside the head, in the middle of the head, I would say the pineal gland region.

A crawling sensation was felt on the forehead, arms, legs, and chest.

At some point, I felt the energy moving stronger in the Muladhara and spiraling up. With this came a little bit of arousal. The images of different lingams were popping into my head, making the arousal even bigger. This took some time, and the energy pushing moved to the head, and arousal disappeared.

In the Anahata, the region was a heavy pounding sensation – as if there was a pendulum inside of it, with energy moving from left to right, underneath both breasts. The pounding sensation also moved to Ajna chakra. Later, I felt intense pain in the Ajna and Anahata regions instead of pounding.

¼ of the sadhan I spent in a deep meditative state – deep inside myself, not feeling the body, gravity, space, or time. Just bliss.

In the end, I felt the solid electric current starting in the middle of the back and going up to the bottom of the head (where the spine connects to the skull), pushing against this spot. And in the end came the pain again – in Ajna the most, then some in the Anahata region too.

I practiced for 2 hours and 30 minutes.

The electric currents didn't disappear completely. I still feel some now – the wrists, the top of the head. They keep coming and going.

My response: Please note that this process will go on over a prolonged period. In my case, the same kind of kriyas went on for years, around 4 or 5 years. But there is simply nothing to worry about it at all. No harm will come to you, either physically or mentally. Please continue with your sadhan the same way but without offering any resistance to the unfolding kriyas, including sex-related thoughts. You should also remember that it is a very long journey. Slowly and steadily, the mind will undergo the necessary transformation.

Question: A practitioner: Throughout the day, as usual – crown activation, electric currents on the top of the head but also on the forehead, micro-explosions in the head, and some vibrations in the Muladhara.

Kriyas started immediately as I closed my eyes. There were repeating patterns of movement as usual – bending of the body with the head to the left and right, small circular movements of the head, more prominent circular movements of the head and some head pulling to the right and left, and head nodding.

The protagonist in the sadhan was again the electric current – on the top of the head, with various intensities, the whole body was electrified again, having kind of a field around it. There was a strong crawling sensation on the arms, head, forehead, and chest. The crown felt intensively electrified, with many concentrated currents. There was a burning sensation on the top of the head and on the back of the head.

Micro-explosions were happening with tremendous intensity – at some point, all over the head. It was many points at once, and a concentrated stream in the back of the head.

In the middle of the head, but slightly to the back, one more significant current was "popping" very strongly. It was around the region of the pineal gland. It felt even as if someone was pounding there with a tiny hammer, and it was also making explosive noise. It repeated rhythmically for a long time.

At some point, the whole head had currents and explosive sounds and a burning sensation on the top, becoming even more disturbing, and the head was itchy.

There was a small electric wave that appeared in the Muladhara, and the constant vibration – spiral energy movement in the body. I strongly felt the spiral, vibrational movement in Vishuddha chakra, Manipura, and Ajna.

Between all those kriyas the body was stopping and I was going deep into a meditation state. My body was disappearing. I didn't feel it or feel gravity, time, or space.

At the end of this sadhan came various pains – first in the Svadhisthana, then Manipura, and then intense pain in Ajna chakra. I also felt pushed going from Muladhara to Svadhisthana, and this pushing gave me even more pain. I also felt exhausted and pumped out of energy in the end.

I practiced for 2 hours and 20 minutes.

Today since the beginning of the day – electric currents have appeared on the top of the head. It seems to be happening every day now.

My response: Okay. Very nice. Please do not worry about the pain at the root and second chakra regions. They do happen sometimes. A few of our lady practitioners also complained about it. The pain should go away after some time.

Question: A practitioner: The kriyas started as soon as I sat to do sadhan. First came the gentle movement of the whole body to the left and right. The circles began to grow in extent and became very big after some time so that the entire body was moving, including the buttocks that were being lifted from the meditation seat.

Next came the movement of throwing arms into the air and back to the floor, which then turned into the worshipping of God movement again. Yesterday afternoon, I stayed in the Dhandawat position for a long time. During this time, various activities came – the first was the movement of a pendulum again, the whole body to left and right, which took a very long time. The burning sensation along the spine came with it, the electric ants on the top of my back and the crown.

The next movement was of the pelvis – it moved to the front and back, with vigorous intensity, and it was also for a long time. Then the head moved in the air without resting the forehead on the floor. The movements interchanged for some time.

I started to hear the running water sound in my left ear – and it became deafening. In the right ear, there was a thunderous low, humming sound pulsating. Both sounds stayed with me till the end of the sadhan.

I pulled back to the sitting position again, and my body started to move like a pendulum, which continued for a long time. Then it turned into circles again. This time the circles were throwing me off the meditation seat in all directions. The arms were landing on the floor and going up at a very high pace. Then I felt the circles were gravitating more to the back, and so I was finally pulled to the back.

I rested in the Savasana position. The first movement was turning the head left and right at a very high pace. Then the legs started to move – left leg turning left, right leg turning right. Then the knees were going up and down, bending and stretching. Then the bended knees joined and started moving to the left and right. Then the feet joined, and knees opened to the sides. Then the hips began to move. In this position, the electric ants on the higher part of my back started to become more intense. The knees got up and started pounding with one another.

After that, the head movement started again – left and right.

I then returned to the sitting position again, and my body started to do the pendulum movement. It changed to enormous circles after a while – this time, my arms were bent, and my elbows were on the floor behind me. After a while, I was more central again, and the vast circles continued. The head joined – the head was moving so dynamically that the hair was going in all directions. It was powerful, and I also started feeling nauseous after a while. The movement then became a pendulum, but the sick feeling continued and became stronger. The vision from yesterday – of the woman who will be burned – came back briefly.

The nausea feeling became so strong that I had to stop the practice. I felt very dizzy in my head as if I was intoxicated. I was also freezing and needed to lie down. I practiced for 1 hour.

On top of my head, the electric current came twice yesterday; during the day, too - when I was riding my bike, it came very strongly but was for a short time. It was very mild during dinner, but I experienced the constant feeling.

My response: Kundalini energy is either awakened or stabilized after Shakthipat initiation. In your case, since it was already in an awakened state, it will now get stabilized slowly and steadily. However, you are safe now. Therefore, there is nothing to worry about it at all. You need to continue with your practice the same way regularly.

Secrets of Shaktipat and Kundalini Yoga

Question: A practitioner: I sat in the sadhan session for around 40 min. I felt a strong gush of energy moving in my whole body. Like the body will blast, body and neck movements are quite strong. There was a strange blackness everywhere. Nowadays, I am sitting in sadhan without any support. One doubt Guru Ji. I am not clear as to whether the thoughts are arising on their own or whether I am thinking about all these. But the session is really peaceful.

My response: Excellent! Try to sit for a longer duration; eventually, it will improve by itself. Thoughts arising during sadhan are kriyas only. You may not be thinking deliberately. It is very common, and you just have to sit in a state of witness, observing them in your mind. Let the thoughts rise; soon, they will vanish also. Chant your mantra mentally and concentrate on your Guru's picture simultaneously.

Question: A practitioner: Sharing my last night's experience in sadhan. I experienced several kriyas of forward bending, and my body remained still in that position for approximately 30 minutes. I experienced a vision of brilliant radiance all throughout the sadhan. Mainly I experienced subtle kriyas of rotations and swinging at the beginning. At one point, I was lying, gazing at the brilliant radiance for a while. Then again, I was back in sitting posture, and only my left eye opened up for a second and was shut again.

Throughout the sadhan, I experienced an outburst of high energy with feelings of chills from my heart region and spreading all over my body. I heard sounds from Heart, Throat, and Sacral Chakras one after another in a sequence. I experienced currents and pain in the heart, feet, palms, stomach, neck, and back regions. Then again, kriyas started with rotations, bending, swinging left to the right, and back and forth. My neck was moving aggressively like a spring in a forward and backward motion.

The duration of sadhan was 4 hrs. Whole day, I was aware of kriyas, like sensations of currents flowing, crawling, and pain in my hands, stomach, ribs, feet, and neck. On some days, I experience a sudden onset of depression, especially after waking up, when I am still in bed in the early morning hours between 5:30 AM to 6:30 AM. Please guide.

My response: Please don't bother about the depression you are experiencing. That is also kriya only. Please remember that kriyas will manifest in the physical body and the other four sheaths. So far, this is the first time you are reporting about the kriyas in Manomaya Kosha or the sheath of mind. Obviously, you will undergo the full range of emotions as kriyas. Just keep observing them like a mute spectator.

Although depression is an unpleasant kriya, you must allow it to manifest without resisting it. Just surrender yourself entirely to the divinity or the cosmic energy. However, in case you feel like kriyas are unbearable concerning the pain you are experiencing. Please stop doing sadhan temporarily for a day or two. That is all you need to do. Otherwise, experiencing brilliant radiance is a good kriya.

Kriyas during sleep

Question: A practitioner: My apologies if this doubt has already been answered. I am unable to recall. Does kriya occur while somebody is asleep?

My response: Karmas are not destroyed during the sleep state. Therefore, while awakened kundalini is active, cleaning karmas per se doesn't happen. However, sleep cycles are strictly controlled by the awakened kundalini energy. Therefore, although kriyas go on around the clock, it is said that karmas are not destroyed. Various other types of cleaning pertaining to the internal body go on.

Manifestation of kriyas

Question: A practitioner: I have a few questions about our Shaktipat. When kriya is slow to materialize, are we to do anything to make fertile ground for kriya to happen? Or just keep chanting the mantra apart from the daily meditation without expectation?

Secondly, how can we deal with situations like family problems and financial distress? Will these happen as per our destiny? While we put in our efforts as we are programmed to, do we have to ultimately reconcile and witness our destiny unfolding as per the divine will? Is our only task to practice daily meditation, having come onto this path?

My response: If you had read my book properly, the abovementioned issues would have been apparent. I have also requested sadhaks to read the compiled questions and answers. The book has already been shared with you all. That book would have cleared most of the routine questions. You are asking me the same basic questions and concepts piecemeal. Nevertheless, I will definitely explain it once again.

There is nothing to be done in our path for the manifestation of kriyas. Because they are instigated to manifest in your body only through the grace or will of your Guru! Therefore, it is suggested that every time you sit for sadhan, focus on your Guru and the given mantra, which has been charged with Shaktipat. Other than this, there is no other technique that can help you in the manifestation of kriyas. You need to surrender yourself entirely to the divine or Guru. As simple as that! Kundalini energy is the supreme cosmic power that is all conscious. Therefore, how can anyone do something to enhance its impact?

The only thing you are supposed to do, and you can do, is to SURRENDER YOURSELF TO THE POWER. In a nutshell, not to do anything! That is the bottom line. Regarding your worldly problems, they are only reflections of your internal karmas. Rather everything you experience is the reflection of your own inner self only. Nothing can be done to avoid karma other than burning it down completely. This is possible only by experiencing it. However, Shaktipat helps minimize the impact in terms of intensity. Lastly, also remember that everything else also gets minimized after Shaktipat. Both your good merits and sins! Therefore, please be prepared for both.

Kriyas related to light

Question: A practitioner: Sharing my last night experiences in sadhan. It lasted for about 4 hrs and 15 minutes. There were kriyas of forward bending, the body became straight, and bright yellow light started appearing. Then again, my body started rotating, stopping, and bright yellow light appeared. Then only bright yellow light was visible and got magnified all over. After a while, my arms got stretched, and I felt as if my whole body was Sunbathing in the bright yellow light. My body was becoming colder and colder. Occasionally, my entire body was swinging left to right, bending back and forth and rotating while focusing on the bright yellow light. On the spine, near the heart Chakra, there were movements, and over the back of the neck, also some currents flowing.

My response: Excellent; the experience of getting surrounded by the light all around is a very good kriya. I am delighted to see your progress. Please continue with your practice the same way. Just remain focused on your sadhan in the same manner. You will start seeing significant benefits in terms of the transformation of your mind.

Touch related kriyas

Question: A practitioner: I am doing regular sadhan, and kriyas are regularly manifesting. I am experiencing new vibrations in the lower part of my eye and ear. I had a strange experience today around 4:00 AM; I felt the presence of someone in my room. I was about to wake up from sleep when someone touched my ankle. I could not understand what to do. I opened my eyes and found no one.

My response: There is nothing unique about it. If you have been following the experiences of our practitioners, a few of them had a similar type of kriyas. There is nothing to worry. They are happening to clean your karma only. Just be brave. If you are thinking about any spirits or demons, please don't worry about it at all. After Shaktipat, a practitioner is protected by the awakened kundalini energy provided sadhan is going on regularly. That is all you need to do. I understood it must have been a little scary, kriya, for you. But such kriyas are also necessary for you. That is how your fear-related karma will get cleaned up. You need to simply endure it like any other uncomfortable kriyas.

Rare type of kriyas

Question: A practitioner: Last night I woke up to an electric shock in both my ears simultaneously, which was quite painful. Guru Ji, are you aware of such a kriya happening?

My response: Very nice. I have not come across this kind of kriya. Nevertheless, it appears to be a kriya only because kriyas are known to manifest in different ways.

Kriyas on Ajna Chakra

Question: A practitioner: Today, I realized that the part between my eyebrows keeps itching. I am not able to wear a tilak on my third eye, be it a roli or bindi.

It was not skin itching or so. Yet I want that third eye area to be natural without anything applied to that area. Why does this happen, Guru Ji!? This has been happening for more than 10-15 years or so. I request your guidance on this.

My response: Very nice. I am happy to hear about your experiences. Yes, they are kriyas only happening at Ajna chakra. They are a little uncomfortable. You need to endure them, but I am very happy for you. Please continue with your sadhan the same way.

Question: A practitioner: I have had a headache for three days, sometimes mild and hectic. It started when I felt a heavy energy on my Ajna chakra and my head while doing sadhan. Should I stop or continue doing it?

My response: That must be some sort of heaviness kind of thing. It may not be a headache in the classical sense. You can take a temporary break for a day or two. But there is nothing to worry about it. Whenever the awakened kundalini energy faces strong opposing karma, this kind of kriya is usually experienced.

Emotions as kriyas

Question: A practitioner: Is getting angry and spilling out anger a kriya?

I am getting much angry with my husband. And it is kind of I am letting out everything. But it is hurting him. Will this be karma? But Guru Ji! I am bursting out like never before.

My response: After a few weeks of regular sadhan mind starts becoming sensitive. Then sadhaks start expressing anger toward the family members, usually or employees if working in an organization. But the awakened kundalini energy will ensure that it happens as a kriya. It usually gets accumulated as fresh karma because sadhak will not be able to exercise adequate dispassion during such moments of intense emotional expression. But such freshly accumulated karma will not be strong enough. It is easier to clear them later on during sadhan. But one shouldn't resist too much either.

Shaktipat

Theoretical questions on Shaktipat

Question: A practitioner: Does the presence of a yogi (Shaktipat practitioner) have influence over others in the family, workplace, etc.? Is it possible, Guru Ji?

My response: No, please. Shaktipat is strictly your private business.

Question: Same practitioner: What influence can a yogi make in society and others' life only by his presence?

My response: I asked this same question to a great man long ago. In the interiors of remote Himalayan ranges! It was suggested by my own Guru ji to ask this question to that great man. His Holiness said its impact is limited since it is a private business. However, he further went on to say that a yogi can light up a million lamps without losing his brilliance. Therefore, that is what a yogi can do. His mere presence may not have much impact. It will be minimal if it is a single lamp, but a million lamps can have a considerable effect. I hope you got the idea now.

Question: A practitioner: I honestly didn't feel anything after or during initiation?

My response: Okay, please don't bother about it. The cosmic energy is too subtle in its primordial form. What people experience are the kriyas or reactions when they start manifesting. This depends upon prevailing psychic conditions. If not now, they will manifest later. Since it is a divine power, it can't be predicted like we do with gross energies in a scientific lab. Please do not focus your mind in that direction at all. The cosmic power is conscious and all-knowing. It will shower its blessings only when the yoga practitioner exercises self-surrender to it from the bottom of the heart. Otherwise, it will not manifest its impact just to satisfy the curiosity of a practitioner. This is very important to note. A practitioner can't fool God or cosmic power.

Shaktipat system

Question: A practitioner: Is our path Jnana Yoga or Karma Yoga?

My response: Ours is not an independent yoga system. However, all yoga systems culminate into our path after the awakening of kundalini energy in a practitioner. That is why our path is called Mahayoga or the grand path. This is not meant for everyone like it happens in other independent yoga systems. It is intended for those who have already reached a particular stage in their spiritual evolution, either in their past or current life. Usually, those persons are destined to come to our path. It happens automatically as per their destiny.

That is why our path is more of a stage in spiritual evolution rather than an independent yoga system. In our path, everything that applies to independent yoga systems like Ashtanga Yoga or Raja Yoga, Bhakti Yoga, Karma Yoga, and also Jnana Yoga is equally important and applicable except the preparatory stages. The only catch is that a practitioner doesn't need to put in the voluntary effort. Everything is naturally happening to them, provided the practitioner does nothing. Therefore, to remain in this state of being a silent spectator and not do anything, a practitioner needs to sit in a meditative posture. I said sitting for sadhan is more of a formality than a technical requirement.

After a practitioner reaches certain levels, every moment of life, whether during sadhan or otherwise, becomes sadhan only. I am surprised that you still have this doubt. I have elaborated on this in my book, also. Lastly, remember that our path is akin to graduating from high school to college. Obviously, all that is learned at school will no longer be relevant, yet some knowledge is certainly applicable. The same is the case here. I hope your doubt is clear now.

Shaktipat deekshadhikara

Question: A practitioner: I feel you have given Shaktipat deekshadhikara to people with very little knowledge. Is it not better to give the mantra first and, after observation for a few months, then give Shaktipat deeksha? Have I spoken out of turn?

My response: Please leave the decision to His Holiness Swami Sahajanand Tirtha. Whatever deekshadhikara I am giving is as per the directions of His Holiness only. I suggest you, please, don't bother about it at all. As I said earlier, if a person has received Shaktipat deekshadhikara, it doesn't mean that he or she is spiritually higher than others.

Someone becoming a Shaktipat Guru is as per their karma only. That will be their sadhan. Moreover, it involves a lot of responsibility. To tell you the truth, I was never interested in becoming a Shaktipat Guru initially. My Guru ji, His Holiness, has repeatedly insisted I honor the decision. Otherwise, I would have been happily alone, focused only on my sadhan.

Question: A practitioner: What are the qualifications, prerequisites, qualities, and attainments required in a Shaktipat practitioner to obtain Dheekshadhikara (The permission to initiate another into the Shaktipat)?

My response: No qualifications. It is all due to blessings from the supreme cosmic power. It is destiny, or it happens as per the karmic balance. It doesn't mean that the person who has received Shaktipat Deekshadhikara is more outstanding than others spiritually. It is more of Guru seva or service to Guru.

Further, it involves a lot of responsibility for the person given Shaktipat Deekshadhikara. That is all about it. I refused to accept Deekshadhikara from my Guru ji His Holiness Swami Sahajanand Tirtha for a long time. Ultimately, I had to accept it due to my own karmic balance. That is all about it. Please don't focus your mind too much on this.

Question: A practitioner: How does a Guru decide who'll carry forward the lineage?

My response: It happens as per destiny, usually serious sadhaks surface in a natural way. Some of you will be chosen for this sacred task in the future. However, there is a catch here: practitioners selected for this sacred duty need not necessarily be the most advanced spiritually. It will eventually be a sadhan for the practitioners chosen as Gurus, as it is more of a responsibility and additional burden for the practitioners. I hope you got the idea now. Guru seva (service) can be done in any manner, not necessarily by carrying forward the lineage. Exactly, it is really very difficult to say how practitioners are chosen.

On my part, I have left it to the supreme cosmic power itself. After all, it is my sadhan also. Actually, my Guru ji, His Holiness Swami Sahajanand Tirtha, has directed me to write a book on the science of giving Shaktipat deeksha for the benefit of future Shaktipat Gurus. Obviously, the subject will also cover the aspect of how to pass on the deekshadhikara or how to choose future Gurus. So, this book needs to address two different themes; one on the topic of giving Shaktipat deeksha and the other on the issue of choosing the future Gurus. Right now, I am involved only in the first part.

Therefore, I don't have adequate knowledge to write even the first part of this book. One day, it may see the light by the grace of my Guru ji, His Holiness. Hence, I don't have much idea regarding your above question about the book's second part.

Impact on external life after Shaktipat

Question: A practitioner: In the last two days, I feel my practice has bled over into other parts of my life. So, I am finding that when I am driving, sitting still, lying down, or reading or seeing a particular narrative, I become aware of physical kriyas. I have also had some old positive memories pop up in the last two days.

There were times when I was happy. And for me, this is interesting because when I first spoke to Guru Ji, I felt like I was living a story that I was very tired of. And right after initiation, I had an insight into certain "negative" karmic themes in my life. So, being reminded of some of the bright episodes in the story was unexpected. But then, I thought that this was also karma. Good and bad sides to the balance sheet. And that this karma is also being cleaned. F

And this has been accompanied by a burning at my heart Chakra. And when I thought this, I was afraid I would lose these memories. But then I realize that even these things are ephemeral and that the memories will last as long as this incarnation lasts. But the deconstruction of the karma associated with them is what is going on.

I am finding exciting insights and connections among the kriyas. Still, the tendency towards the analytical is a feature of this mind. Is this karma also being purged? So, right now, I feel like I could say something almost every day. And I may be sharing too much.

My response: Everything gets impacted comprehensively after Shaktipat initiation. This includes your intellect, mind, body, and external world. In this connection, let me remind you that the external world you undergo is a projection of what is accumulated in your subconscious mind as karma. Therefore, there is nothing strange about your experiences. These will go on over a prolonged period, thus affecting the cleaning of your karmas.

Question: A practitioner: I rarely practice sadhan and rarely experience kriyas. But what disturbs me is my overactive mind; that I cannot do well with my peers. This is probably because of my past karma. I feel like all the wrong things I did to my peers in the past are being done to me. Please, Guru Ji, is there a mantra for repentance of my past sins? Please guide me into this.

My response: Please understand that whatever you are undergoing is due to your past karmas or actions. Those must be either from past lives or current life. After Shaktipat initiation, those karmas will start getting neutralized. As a result, there will be a holistic change in your life.

You will start attaining real peace of mind and happiness. It is a continuous process. But for this, you need to practice meditation regularly. Otherwise, if you depend on mantras to solve your problems, they will become new karmas for you.

The science of mantra is as materialistic as any other physical science, although it developed in ancient times. That means you must also practice the mantra over a prolonged period, even to attain materialistic benefits. However, you will end up wasting a lifetime. Whether that mantra will be fruitful for you at the earliest or not can't be predicted. You are a mature man and an educated man. I hope you understand what I am trying to say.

If you are seeking some supernatural powers to come to your rescue, please also understand what will happen to your accumulated karma in your subconscious mind. Therefore, from this perspective, Shaktipat is the best option for you. It will reduce the impact of your karma and clean them for you at a rapid pace. Of course, both your good and bad karma will get wiped out. Isn't this the best option for you?

Please understand this, exercise full self-surrender to the divinity, and practice meditation. In any case, I don't deal with the science of mantras meant for materialistic benefits. It is a different yoga practice. I have no idea about it. The mantra I have given you was meant for a different purpose. To transfer the cosmic energy to your body and awaken the kundalini energy! This has already been done in your body.

All that you need to do is allow it to work. That means just sit for meditation and do nothing! Do nothing other than focus your mind on your Guru and the mantra. As simple as that! I hope you have some clarity on this subject now.

My response: It is your own karma intertwined with life events. As your karmas start getting destroyed, so is the external life, which gets affected. Obviously, your family members are nothing but extensions of your life.

Question: A practitioner: I wanted to know that despite experiencing the kundalini energy. Is doing the sadhan enhancing anything? Also, are the visions or images we may see related to oxygen in the brain?

My response: I don't understand the first question correctly. Sitting in sadhan means not formally doing anything, so the awakened kundalini energy cleans karmas. While the karmas are cleaned, the impact is felt as kriyas. Otherwise, how can anyone experience the kundalini energy? One can't even experience the grosser energies while undergoing medical checks like x-rays, MRI scans, etc.

Kundalini energy is so subtle. It is purely Maya or the illusion. Its nature can't be comprehended by human intellect. It has to reveal itself. Therefore, I have answered both the points raised in this question about experiencing kundalini energy and sadhan. What else is expected? You are under the impression that some of your sensory skills will be enhanced or attain supernatural powers. Obviously, they manifest at later stages in samadhi. But a practitioner is not supposed to focus on achieving them because it is a strict taboo for spiritual growth.

The moment the mind is focused on attaining supernatural powers, spiritual growth immediately stops, followed by a dangerous fall.

Regarding the second question, images or visions are kriyas only. They are the accumulated sensual impressions or karmas from the subconscious mind. But their relationship with the presence of oxygen in the brain is an irreverent question.

Oxygen is a gross physical substance. It is part of the element air. How can this be compared to the cleaning of karmas in the form of images and visions?

Karma, creation, illusion and scriptures

Theoretical questions on creation

Question: A practitioner: I am reading the book 'Secrets of Shaktipat' and have read up to page 63. There are a few doubts that I was wondering about from what I have read so far.

Vedas mention that God said, "may I be many." Are the Vedas or any other sacred source or Guru Ji's insights also tell us why God wished it this way. Is there any reason? I think even the search, for this reason, is illusionary? But why was this illusion created in the first place?

Seeking knowledge about the workings of the universe etc., is also an illusion (as per a question asked by a sadhak). But can we continue to gain knowledge as a part of being in the 3D world and yet avoid making karma?

If there is no other entity but just me (page 45). Then does this mean we are all one? If yes, then is the ascension of one interrelated to the ascension of others? And, is vice versa also true?

Colonel T Sreenivasulu

My response: Let me start answering you in the same sequence. First, I suggest you finish reading the book on questions and answers. As you keep reading it, your doubts will be cleared piecemeal. Otherwise, I will repeat the same answers again and again. Notwithstanding this, I understand that you may have specific queries unique to you. Definitely, I will be happy to answer all your questions.

Para 1. You are trying to understand the concept within the parameters of limited intellect. As long as you exist in dualism, these questions are relevant. But the answers to these questions are outside the realm of rational explanation. For example, you had a dream yesterday night. You were a philosopher in the dream. You were pondering over some problems about the phenomenon of life. You were involved in heated discussions with partners from your dream world. But upon waking, you realize that all that heated discussion you had in your dream world is simply an illusion. Nothing was ever real. Neither you as the philosopher in the dream nor the partners nor the discussion! However, it must have been very real to you while the dream lasted for you. That is the crux of the story. Everything gets resolved internally as your mind undergoes the transformation during sadhan. You start getting the answers to everything from within.

Para 2. How can you gain knowledge of the 3D world when that knowledge is simply illusionary in existence? It is akin to theorizing about the existence of water in a desert in the form of a mirage. For example, two people are standing in a desert. A local illiterate person and a scientist who happens to be a tourist! They both see water at a distance in the form of a mirage. Both know the truth. However, the scientist gives his masterly exposition for why such an illusion is being created. Whereas the illiterate person simply says why are you wasting your time. I know that there is no water there. Therefore, what is the knowledge you are seeking? It may be suitable for writing a book or lecturing someone. Otherwise, it is not even classified as knowledge. The awareness that a mirage in a desert is not water is knowledge.

Para 3. Yes, there is simply one spirit pervading the entire cosmos. Call it by whichever name you wish. However, the idea of a Godhead is akin to a circle whose center is nowhere to be found and whose circumference is infinity. Whereas in the case of an individual person, the center is located within the self, but again, the circumstance is infinite. However, spiritual evolution results in the self-realization that you are God. Its implication will be the realization that " you " exists in every creature. However, the rest of the world goes on. Because it is "you" as the God who created all those creatures by your divine will saying, "MAY I BE MANY." So, whom will you blame for their misery now?

Moksha for animals

Question: A practitioner: I would like to ask you a question about animals. What about my dogs? How would they move towards their ascension? Everything I have been studying, from psychology to healing modalities, now seems questionable, and this is making me experience a lot of inertia in my mind. That is why there are so many questions.

My response: The mechanism for self-realization exists only in the human body. That is the reason it is referred to as the miniature model of the cosmos. In the case of animals, first, the transmigration needs to occur to the human form. Please understand that animals you see around might have been previously born as humans. Similarly, some humans you see around now might degenerate into animals in the future. But this phenomenon is temporary.

The spirit pervading all creatures makes the general ascent from the state being a mineral to man. However, after achieving human birth in millions of eons, it doesn't necessarily remain human until self-realization is completed. It might slip back or degenerate into animal wombs and also vice versa. A similar fate applies to even celestial beings and subterranean beings who exist in other planes. So, none is spared. Ultimately, it is human birth alone in which it is possible to begin a yoga practice.

Therefore, the transmigration of the creatures is the key. The reason for the increase in human population on the planet is also this same transmigration. Otherwise, where do you think all these extra people are being born? Certainly, they have not been created by God all of a sudden. Some animals would have got upgraded to human status. A similar fate is awaited for some humans in a reverse manner, depending on their karmas.

Of course! I can't say anything about the current status of your dog, please. All those sciences you have been studying pertain to materialistic things. They have nothing to do with spiritual growth. Therefore, please delink all that literature from your sadhan. If you wish, you can continue with your pursuit of all that you have been doing to earn your bread. However, for your personal salvation, do sadhan! This spiritual knowledge is strictly your private business. It has no benefit for anyone else.

Creating karma

Question: A practitioner: Do thoughts also make karmas or is it just outward action that makes them?

My response: Any thought, word, or deed tinged with egoism is deemed karma.

Karma related issues

Question: A practitioner: Isn't the desire for moksha or wanting spiritual ascension also karma since we are doing it with an expectation of the consequence?

My response: Actually, as long as a person is in a state of dualism, all such questions and discussions on them take place. After one starts to enter into a state of non-dualism, which is the final journey obviously, there is no more such idea left. Only in the initial stages do these ideas pop up in your mind. Of course, it is karma only. Any thought or word, or deed tinged with egoism is karma. But these karmas are unavoidable. Without a desire for moksha, one can't begin the yoga practice.

Similarly, eating food is also karma. But we still perform those karmas because body maintenance is impossible otherwise. Therefore, while living within the parameters of Maya or the cosmic illusion, one needs to rise above it.

Kriya and karma

Question: A practitioner: How does one know if it is a kriya or simply an event in life? I know that we get kriyas while sitting with our mantra etc. But yesterday, after my 2nd morning, I took a nap, and upon waking from my nap, my once-perfect wrist had pretty severe pain in it. I am just wondering about that. Is that a kriya, or did I merely lay on it wrongly?

My response: There is a fragile line of difference between kriya and karma. For example, if you move your hand deliberately, it is karma. If it moves involuntarily during practice, then it is called kriya. When gross physical kriyas manifest, these are easily identified. Sometimes, kriyas are so violent that you have no doubt regarding them. However, when subtle kriyas manifest, this sort of doubt keeps arising. But this is only in the initial stages of your practice. You shall get the necessary understanding that they are kriyas.

For example, kriyas can happen as emotional outbursts also. Suddenly, your mind may jump into a fit of rage at someone. It may get triggered by a minor thought that has suddenly risen in your mind. Similarly, other emotional outbursts can also arise about various subjects like humor, compassion, courage, etc. These emotions are experienced by an ordinary person also. But there will be a marked difference in the experience. When it is a kriya, it is more playful in nature. It will not bind you with fresh karma. However, the difference will be subtler when kriyas are not grosser. I suggest you please read my book "Secrets of Shaktipat and Kundalini Yoga." It is a compilation of several questions and answers done over some time.

Theoretical questions on karma

Question: A practitioner: If everything happens by divine free will, why does God make us do negative karma? Does God make us do it, or do we do it ourselves?

My response: There is no negative karma or positive karma in the eyes of God. It exists only in human understanding. It is akin to various other opposites like heat and cold. Do you really think God feels cold or heat? Or does he know the difference between bitter and sweet? Therefore, your above question needs to be understood comprehensively and not in isolation. In any case, human intellect or the rational thinking faculty has limited capabilities. Please don't rely on that. Instead, surrender yourself entirely if you wish to seek true knowledge.

Surrender involves body, mind, and intellect, not simply your body or mind. Unfortunately, most people do it with their bodies by folding their hands or kneeling in front of the altar. A few intelligent people do it with their minds also in addition to their bodies. They think that they can outsmart God by using their brilliant intellect. However, if you surrendered your intellect to God, you wouldn't have asked the above question. Because the above question is within the realm of intellect tinged with egoism. I hope you understand the concept now.

Illusionary existence

Question: A practitioner: This urge to understand more and more is continuing. I had discussed the topic of the Law of Attraction the moment I met you. I also discussed Pranic Healing. The topic "Everything is Energy" is a part of your book. I had read the book with the expectation that I would

Secrets of Shaktipat and Kundalini Yoga

learn more energy-related manifestation techniques. You helped me understand that there is nothing like a materialistic world; everything is energy. I have undergone many changes in me after taking deeksha from you. I do not fear anymore. I can look at things from a new perspective. However, when I think of doing meditation, kundalini sadhan, I am not able to carry out the intention. I always face some obstacles. Please excuse me if I am wrong.

My response: It seems your mind is focused on the materialistic aspects. Everything in this world is energy, and energy means simply ILLUSIONARY. That means It is not TRUE. When you feel that there is something when there is nothing, that is called ILLUSION. It is akin to a mirage in a desert or mistaking a rope for a snake in the darkness.

Therefore, all your inner desires in this illusionary world will start vanishing as you progress on the path of yoga. As far as your intellectual reasoning or understanding is concerned, that is also illusionary only. That is the reason why you are getting this doubt in your mind. LIFE is basically illusionary in nature, akin to a dream world. In a state of samadhi, this starts to disintegrate, just like a dream disintegrates when you wake up from sleep. This needs to be EXPERIENCED.

You cannot comprehend it intellectually because there is a limitation to the human intellect. It is not the supreme form of cosmic energy. It is like a denser or gross form of cosmic energy. Therefore, how can a grosser thing comprehend a subtler thing? It is akin to saying you need a finer needle or instrument to remove a thorn in your flesh. Obviously, you can't remove it by using a thick wooden tool. I hope you get the idea now. I have explained all these issues right at the beginning of my book. Kindly read it once again.

Samadhi, Anahata sound, dispassion, self-surrender, mantras, food habits, service to Guru, renunciation

Samadhi

Question: A practitioner: Once the thoughtless state is attained, there will be no sense of me or time. It is just awareness. So, this state is Samadhi? And if this state is permanent, is it moksha?

My response: Reaching a thoughtless state or Samadhi is not like jumping into a well suddenly. It is akin to entering into ocean waters. First, you enter the shallow waters. Slowly you enter into the depths. Once you enter it thoroughly, there is no coming back either. Similarly, you start entering into lower states of Samadhi first, and that too for little time. Slowly, a practitioner develops the ability to remain in the state of Samadhi for longer and longer.

However, awareness of the self is very much present during such states of lower Samadhi. But this is not moksha since you are still in a state of dualism. What happens after that is not known. Even the ancient texts have remained silent after that. Technically the objective of yoga would have been achieved by entering into the lower Samadhi. That is the terminal objective of all yoga systems and philosophies. But that is a very high state from a spiritual point of view. Although one can slip down and fall back even from such a high spiritual state. That means even that state is not permanent. That is the state to which a practitioner is taken to, by the awakened kundalini energy.

After that, the character of the final journey for salvation changes dramatically as per the ancient texts. But they remained silent on such a journey. It can be comprehended that it is futile to even try to imagine such a state from worldly logic. It is akin to trying to comprehend infinity or God by imagination. How is it possible? Therefore, please don't get distracted by all such thoughts. Please focus on your sadhan only.

Question: A practitioner: What are Samadhi and Enlightenment?

My response: Samadhi is a thoughtless state. But the idea of dualism still exists in lower samadhi. The sense of I'ness is still there. The final journey begins from lower samadhi towards a state of self-realization, moksha, enlightenment, etc. Non-dualism with God is realized.

Samadhi is broadly categorized into two stages. All yoga texts speak of savikalpa samadhi or samprajnata samadhi or lower samadhi, wherein dualism is still experienced. However, it is a very high state. As per yoga texts, even supernatural powers may manifest in this mind state.

From this state, the final journey begins to higher samadhi or nirvikalpa samadhi or asamprajnata samadhi, etc. Enlightenment is not our terminology. It is more of a Buddhist language, I suppose. It probably means the same as higher samadhi.

Question: A practitioner: I am sorry, but I felt like I have to ask. What is the final outcome? What happens if "kriyas fully happening"?

I read many of these sensations: electric, tingling, strange body/head movements, etc. What is the final benefit of all of these? Is anyone here who passed these signals and awakened his /her kundalini? And what is life for him?

My response: After Shakthipat initiation, the accumulated karmas or the sensual impressions in the subconscious mind start getting destroyed. That impact is experienced as different kriyas. The effect is felt in the intellect, mind, body, and external lifestyle. As karmas are cleaned, the kriyas also start slowing down and become subtler and subtler.

After some years of practice, every moment of life is experienced as a kriya only. As a result of all this cleaning of karma, the mind undergoes lots of internal transformation. A practitioner starts enjoying inner peace and bliss. In later stages, the mind begins entering into samadhi, or the thoughtless state. Even the supernatural powers themselves are supposed to get manifested at higher levels. However, what happens after that or whether a merger with God is affected can't be predicted by anyone. Even the ancient yoga texts have remained silent on this subject. But reaching samadhi itself is an outstanding achievement.

Innumerable sages worldwide have struggled to reach such a state since immemorial. All these details have been repeated by me very often. Practitioners need to read the pdf on questions and answers. Most of their doubts will get answered as such. Otherwise, answering each practitioner individually and on the same repeated questions becomes difficult. Instead, the practitioner can focus his mind on other new issues.

It is unfair for the practitioners to ask questions without reading the pdfs they have been told to read. Notwithstanding the above, please be advised that if practitioners expect any materialistic benefits from Shaktipat initiation, then this path is useless to you.

Secrets of Shaktipat and Kundalini Yoga

This path is purely meant for seeking the grace of the divine by burning down one's karmas or sensual impressions. It is not a quick-fix solution for any materialistic benefits. Practitioners should comprehend that they can't cheat the all-knowing cosmic energy or God. If they think so, then they can leave this path because it will be a waste of time and effort for them.

Anahata sound

Question: A practitioner: Would you consider the tones I am getting in my ears as kriyas?

My response: Yes, please. It is Anahata sound only.

Question: A practitioner: What is the sound of Anahata naad? Is it like, chinnnnnnnnnnnnn?

My response: No. It is usually like the hissing of a snake. However, it takes on different forms as well. Twinkling of bells, humming small bush flies, sometimes like the hiss of a rice pressure cooker, etc. Sometimes like the sound of rainfall even. Why are you asking this now? I thought you had already read my book. I have explained this in detail.

Dispassion and compassion

Question: A practitioner: What is the difference between dispassion and lack of compassion? Should we have karuna (compassion)?

My response: Compassion is one of the nine categories of human emotions. Dispassion is a totally different quality. It is a state of mind wherein a person is not impacted by any of the nine categories of emotions. Therefore, the word dispassion is a class apart. It can't be understood in relation to anything at all.

Question: Same practitioner: When one is dispassionate, one is not impacted internally. I have understood that very clearly. However, does that also mean that showing outward compassion towards someone/others at large should be restrained? To summarise what I am trying to understand. Can one attain dispassion while also being compassionate/humble/ empathetic towards others? Or those two states are contradictory?

My response: It seems there is a little confusion in understanding the issue. As I said, dispassion is a state of mind. Compassion happens to be just one of the human emotions. For example, a person in a state of near-perfect dispassion may be exhibiting any of the human emotions in his or her daily life. But due to the fact that he or she is in a state of dispassion, those experiences wouldn't bind the person under the karmic law.

However, please also understand that usually, negative actions are not made to be performed by a person who happens to be in such a high state of dispassion. Usually, whatever such a person does, is meant for the welfare of mankind. But then that person is not bound by such actions either.

Now, coming to your question as to whether that person is restrained from showing compassion to society at large. It is not about being restrained or let loose. It depends upon the karmic balance left. In a nutshell, it depends upon the divine will, whether that person is to be a medium for the benefit of others or not. Otherwise, that person doesn't give a damn about anything; let alone activities arising out of compassion or anything else. These things have been explained in my book also. I request you kindly read it again.

Question: Same practitioner: Will it be okay to say it is emotional detachment. Please correct me if I am wrong. Any action done with emotional detachment incurs less or no karma. For e.g.

1. Assuming a soldier defending the country, he has to shoot the enemy to defend the country. Here he has to have the following state of mind that he is doing it as per the duty required.

2. He should not become happy or sad in his actions

3. He must not be selfish.

4. He should not do it with an end goal. This is also the act of a karma yogi. In fact, it is the goal that evokes emotion.

This is what I perceive. Of course, emotional detachment is not an easy thing to achieve.

My response: I am sorry to say this. Your message is a little messy to understand. It is not straight. Why are you trying to describe the state of mind etc.? Dispassion is a state of mind which can't be explained in earthly languages. That means you can't exercise it deliberately. Then that act itself becomes karma besides being a fake dispassion.

Question: Same practitioner: I understand that it cannot be exercised deliberately. But how can we then get this detachment or the dispassion?

My response: Actually, we both are messing up a simple issue. Human emotions are fuelled by accumulated karma. Otherwise, the human mind's natural state is always that of dispassion. Therefore, as you burn down your karma, you naturally gravitate toward the state of dispassion.

Question: Same practitioner: Isn't this the central theme in the Bhagavad-Gita? Just asking?

My response: Yes, please.

Question: Same practitioner: Yes. This is very clear. In fact, this is short and concise but profound. That means we just continue the sadhan. Up to this point, I can understand. Just one more doubt. You have often said not to desire/expect the kriyas to happen. It will manifest on its own at the right time. You also said to expect or fake the kriyas will result in new karma. That means I should always be mindful that I do the sadhan without getting attached to my emotions. It could also mean I should disregard or not concentrate on the emotions. Am I right in understanding this part?

My response: It doesn't happen that easily, as you suggest. Intellectually what you say is okay. But practically, you tend to get carried away by the rising emotions. Just go with the flow. You will not be able to exercise your mind adequately during such moments, let alone the dispassion. I have mentioned several times that fresh karma accumulated, as a result, will not be that strong. It is relatively easier to clear them later during sadhan.

Therefore, you should focus on going through the emotions as they unfold rather than resisting them. This is crucial to understand. Because sometimes you will get carried away by such emotions that you may NOT BE ABLE TO EVEN IMAGINE IN YOUR WILDEST OF DREAMS. Please understand that this is a yoga practice. You will be tested out to your core. Yoga is not a matter of intellectual amusement or understanding. In a nutshell, you will not be able to do your practice in the manner you suggest above.

Self-surrender

Question: A practitioner: Can you explain the practical way of self-surrender? However, much I try, invariably, I and mine take dominance. So how exactly can surrender happen?

My response: It arises through constant practice. Always focus your mind on your Guru's image. It is one and the same as focusing on the awakened kundalini energy. Since the supreme cosmic power has no form, it is easier to visualize it in the form of the Guru's image. The energy radiates from the physical body of the Guru during Shaktipat deeksha. It enters the body of the person receiving Shaktipat.

The thought of Guru results in the invocation of the cosmic power itself. Therefore, continuously or as many times as possible in a day, focus on your Guru's image! This will start developing as a habit in your mind. This further removes the idea of I'ness in a practitioner whenever karma is done or kriya is experienced. It takes some kind of sincerity on the part of the practitioner.

Secrets of Shaktipat and Kundalini Yoga

Please remember that a person can't fake self-surrender. One needs to be truthful in the heart. Question yourself in the depth of your heart about how sincere you are. You will find the answer for yourself. That is what is meant by going inward instead of going outward into the materialistic world. Please don't worry if you are not able to exercise perfect self-surrender. This is a problem for everyone, including myself.

As long as we live in our human bodies, exercising perfect self-surrender is impossible. In a perfect state of self-surrender, we cease to exist in the human body. Therefore, please don't get too disturbed by your imperfections. Just do whatever you can sincerely from the depths of your heart. The supreme cosmic power, which is conscious, will take care of the rest. It will start guiding you on the correct path.

Question: Same practitioner: If total surrender means accepting EVERYTHING that God gives you, then if God doesn't want you to have Mukti, should I accept that also? Does it mean I will have to wait thousands of lifetimes for God to feel that this is the right time for my Mukti?

My response: Just freeze your mind. Just still your mind. Just surrender your mind. Including the intellect is all you need to do. Just do it by hook or crook. After Shaktipat, it is done by the awakened kundalini energy in any case. You enter into a state of bliss when your mind is still. You will be out of the dimension of your intellect when your mind is in a state of thoughtlessness. What happens after that is not known. Even all the ancient texts have remained silent after that. No great sage or Guru has ever come back to tell the story.

All Yoga systems, tantric methods, philosophies, religions, and if there is anything else, all aim to reach the state of thoughtlessness. Nothing is known that is beyond intellect. Who is God? Where is God? You are that very God. Therefore, where's the question of God granting you moksha or not granting you moksha?

All your above questions have to mean only as long as you are in a state of dualism, thinking that God is a separate Gentleman and YOU are different. That dualism arises in your intellect due to the co-location of your egoism in the same sheath. That is why I mentioned that you need to surrender yourself completely. Surrender your intellect before you start comprehending the true nature of the divine. In a nutshell, you can't understand God with your intellect. I hope the concept is clear now.

Mantras

Question: A practitioner: Why was your mantra changed three times by your Guru, His Holiness Sri Swami Sahajananda Tirthji Maharaj?

My response: A mantra is given to a person by the Guru as per the instructions received by him from his own Guru. It is different for different people. That means the same mantra is not given to all people. Similarly, mantra might be changed to a person depending upon the changes in a person's mental condition, and that too only if required. It entirely depends upon the Guru.

But this kind of knowledge is imparted from Guru to Guru only. It can't be revealed to a person why only a particular mantra was given and why not something else. Similarly, it can't be revealed which mantra will be changed at later stages. Kindly be advised accordingly. Specific tips or techniques Shakthipat Gurus use can't be made public to sadhaks. Such things will be revealed to future Shakthipat Gurus only.

Question: A practitioner: Once the Shakti is active, I thought the mantra is only secondary, or does the mantra play some other role in the process?

My response: Mantra plays a crucial role after Shakthipat deeksha. It is one of the four methods a Guru uses for doing Shakthipat on a person. Therefore, although Shakti remains active after Shaktipat initiation, Shakti is invoked whenever the mantra is chanted. Similarly, whenever a Guru is remembered, Shakti is invoked. Therefore, the mantra, Guru and Shakti, are all one.

Question: A practitioner: Is Pranava a mantra?

My response: My knowledge of mantra sastra, or the science of mantras, is zero. However, in our path, a mantra is used as a vessel, vehicle, or carrier to transfer shakti or the cosmic energy from a Guru to the disciple. Further, it is one of the four methods used. That means There is no need for a Shakthipat Guru to use the mantra compulsorily as such. Just exercising free will is adequate.

However, in our path, we use more than one method just to be over-cautious. This mantra will automatically stop at some stage after the kriyas begin. Hence, it is only a temporary thing. A mantra is essentially used for materialistic benefits by mankind. That is how mantra sastra has been developed since ancient times. One shouldn't compare the mantra chanting like it is done in various other independent yoga systems or tantric systems. Usually, this is the mistake made by many of our sadhaks. They try to compare with other systems.

Shakthipat is a higher yoga technique. Here the mantra has been charged with shakti or cosmic energy before it was given to him. Hence, the mantra itself has no relevance. It is Shakthipat initiation which is of primary importance. Please be advised not to focus on what mantra has been given. There is nothing in the mantra from a spiritual point of view.

As I said earlier, all mantras are meant for materialistic benefits only. It is just a sophisticated science. One needs to exercise self-surrender to the Guru and not focus on the importance of the mantra. Although one needs to chant it regularly.

Regarding the doubt whether Om is a mantra or not or called by some other name doesn't merit any discussion here in view of what I have said above. I am not a Sanskrit scholar on the science of mantras, and I give different mantras to different people as per the directions of Guru parampara. One needs to keep it a secret, of course. Please read my book "The Illusion" for more information regarding the Om mantra.

Service to Guru

Question: A practitioner: You said earlier that the relationship with Guru must also be severed in the end. Not quite clear, please.

My response: Yes, a disciple always does service to his or her Guru. That is the path ordained to seek knowledge of Brahman. It is not possible in any other way other than through a Guru. Please don't get distracted by modern literature.

In modern times, people look upon their Guru simply as a teacher, guide, or mentor. They think that it is all a Guru can do. But in reality, the relationship has much greater depth. Here a person doesn't worship the Guru personally as a human. Instead, it is the Guru tattva that is worshipped. Since the Guru tattva has no form, therefore the Guru is worshipped in the physical form. It is the only way ordained by God to attain moksha through the technique known as Guru. However, this support system in the form of a Guru also needs to end for further progress. Otherwise, attachment to one's Guru will be an obstacle for the practitioner.

Food habits

Question: A practitioner: Will drinking coffee have a negative effect on the Kundalini energy and our sadhan?

My response: After receiving Shaktipat deeksha, there are no restrictions on what you can eat or drink, so, therefore, your coffee question has no bearing on your Kundalini energy.

Question: Same practitioner: I thought of asking this because I heard a Kundalini yoga Guru saying such a few years ago. He said it would affect the flow of Kundalini energy. I now assume he must have been talking about the method he followed and according to his tradition of yogic practices.

My response: In other forms of yoga, like Ashtanga Yoga, this may be the case, but I can't comment. But you have been initiated into the highest form of yoga through Shaktipat. So, these restrictions do not apply. All you have to do is surrender to cosmic energy; that is it.

Renunciation

Question: A practitioner: The soul is eternal and completely dissociated from this material world. Then why do you stress about fulfilling duties again and again? If one knows that the soul is immortal, shouldn't he or she just leave everything and take up the life of a renunciate as Buddha did?

My response: It is called beggar's philosophy. A beggar also says that he has renounced everything in life. That is why he says he has nothing, but that is not called true renunciation.

Question: Same practitioner: Can you elaborate on this, Guru Ji?

My response: First, you be brave. Try not to run away; you can't obtain Moksha without clearing your karmas. In that way, everyone commits all sins and tries to get away free without getting punished. You can't take shelter under the philosophy when it suits you.

If you have acquired any good merits, try to renounce them. Buddha was a great man, born as a prince, married a beautiful princess, and then renounced everything. What do you have to renounce?

Question: Same practitioner: Yes, I understand. But if I have to suffer karma, it can happen anywhere. It needn't be from my home itself.

My response: You can't decide how to get punished. Your punishment is not as per your whims and fancies.

Question: Same practitioner: But Buddha, amidst all this, took the path of a renunciate.

My response: I am asking you a simple question. Buddha had renounced after possessing everything. Don't you see the difference? You only see his actions without factoring in the above. You are called compassionate when you have the power to harm someone but choose not to. What compassion can you show when you don't have any power?

Question: Same practitioner: Okay. But what do you have to say about the life of Shankaracharya?

My response: He already had the required mental condition. Don't you know what happened to him? At such a very young age, he established so many peetas. First, be brave. Renunciation is not meant for those who are not courageous. There is a difference in this.

Most people who want to renounce are basically fake. They don't dare to face the consequences. Renunciation needs a lot of courage and mental dispassion. When a person has such mental dispassion, it doesn't matter whether he lives in a city or a forest. Please understand this carefully. It seems you have no clarity on what renunciation is. It is simply a lifestyle, nothing more than that.

Renunciation doesn't bring you Moksha. Freeing yourself from karmas will surely get you Moksha; this is the message of Krishna in the Gita.

Why didn't Lord Krishana allow Arjun to renounce the war? He was God; Krishna could have won the battle in any case. Moreover, he knew that life was eternal. Then why didn't he allow Arjun to walk away when he decided not to fight the battle? Do you have any answer for this?

Secrets of Shaktipat and Kundalini Yoga

You need to understand this comprehensively. Whereas you are like one of the 11 blind men arguing about what an elephant looks like. One of the blind men holding the tail of an elephant describes the elephant as like a rope. He keeps on arguing endlessly. Therefore, what you say is also true. But then, it is not the complete story.

General topics

Sadhus

Question: A practitioner: What would be the approximate stage of spiritual attainment of those Sadhus who have been doing meditation for many years in the caves of the Himalayas? Please share your views.

My response: It is a very vague question. How will I know about them? I, too, am a sadhak like you struggling to burn down my karmas. Who are those sadhus you are referring to? God only knows who is at which stage? How does it concern you? They are also like you and me, struggling to wash off their karma. Please don't bother too much about such matters. Just focus solely on yourself alone. Wash off your own karma and be free.

Question: Same practitioner: My Apologies. I was just thinking that sitting in such a place as Himalayan caves may help avoid accumulating new karmas while destroying past karmas simultaneously.

My response: There are two kinds of yogis. One category is those who renounce worldly life, wear saffron clothes and live away from mainstream society. The second category is those who live amidst mainstream society and practice yoga.

Secrets of Shaktipat and Kundalini Yoga

Both methods have their advantages and disadvantages. We can't say which is the better method. It depends upon the destiny of the yoga practitioner which path he chooses. I have explained this in my book, also. Please read the concerned chapter once again, if possible.

Question: Same practitioner: I may be asking this question again just to reassure myself. It seems that this path is a grace of God to us who have made some progress in other paths. Just by sitting in the daily sadhan, invoking Gurus' blessings, and letting the divinity do the rest. All of it seems so very easy. We only have to give that much time. The food has been prepared and brought to our mouths due to our previous austerities or divine grace. We just have to open our mouth and gulp it. Is this understanding, correct?

My response: Yes, please. Divine grace is always like that. It is so easily and freely accessible, provided you exercise complete self-surrender. Otherwise, it is not possible to attain it. However, hard you try with your egoism-based attitude. That is the secret of success in yoga; self-surrender. You don't have to go anywhere to seek divine grace. It is showered on you right in your house, provided you seek it sincerely and surrender to it. Shaktipat is there right in front of you as proof.

Question: Same practitioner: Can yogis in our lineage stay in seclusion in the Himalayas? I ask because we are not taught any breathing technique that will increase our inner fire, which yogis in the Himalayas practice to protect them from cold.

My response: That is for people who practice independent yoga systems like Ashtanga Yoga or Raja Yoga. Not required and not applicable to practitioners in our path. Since Shaktipat is Mahayoga, the sadhak learns and practices many of these techniques automatically. For example, khechari mudra is not taught in the Shaktipat tradition as it is a Hathyoga subject. Still, it happens naturally in the Skatipat tradition. Swami Vishnu Thirth ji used to experience Khechari quite frequently during his sadhan days.

On eclipses

Question: A practitioner: Is there any specific guideline or instructions for 21st June during a solar eclipse. Kindly advise!

My response: You all can do sadhan during the eclipse time. It is supposed to be very auspicious for all kinds of yoga practices.

Mental worship

Question: A practitioner: I want to share my experience with you today. In the morning, I did Manas Puja for you. And when I was mentally doing the Puja, it felt as though someone had pressed my forehead where the third eye Chakra is and kept it pressed. My head also felt very heavy. I intended to do the Manas Puja for all the Gurus of our lineage, but somehow, I could only do it for you. Once I finished doing the Puja for you, suddenly, I saw I was doing the Puja for my reiki teacher, and then my eyes opened. This whole sadhan lasted about 30 minutes, but it was quite profound. Once my eyes opened, the feeling of my forehead being pressed went away. My head was still very heavy, and then a bit later, I got a headache which went away sometime in the afternoon.

My response: Mental worship needs practice, also. Please make it a habit first on a regular basis. Otherwise, such events usually do happen. The appearance of your Reiki teacher in your mind was obviously more of an obstacle created for you. In this connection, please also understand why obstacles are created for yoga practitioners in the first place. Kindly read my book on the compiled questions and answers. It is negative karma accumulated by you in the past pertaining to yoga. But no need to worry about it because that also doesn't last permanently! Once an obstacle has been created for you, like it happened today, some negative karma would also have been cleaned up. In the future, please try and cultivate the habit of doing mental worship. If you practice it regularly, then it will naturally come to you.

Gaining weight

Question: A practitioner: I overeat these days. I am gaining weight too. Please Guide.

My response: That is kriya only. It happens that way sometimes. Please don't worry about it too much. However, please try and eat moderately. In my case, I have gained and lost nearly 20 kgs during the last four years. These kinds of fluctuations do take place. Please don't worry. Please try and follow some dietary routines. Soon things might start changing for you. Please give serious thought to what you eat. Avoid everything that adds up to your weight gain. Do everything that helps you lose weight; however small it might be.

Dream related issues

Question: A practitioner: During yesterday evening's sadhan, initially, I felt a powerful energy flow on my head and forehead area. I also experienced pain and heaviness in the center of my chest and sensation in the navel and Muladhara chakra areas. Then after some time, the head pulled back to its maximum 3 times. Then the head was rotated 3 times in clockwise and anticlockwise directions. The sadhan duration was of 75 minutes. After sadhan, I lay down on the bed. Intense sensations were there. I fell asleep, and then a dream started.

In my dream, I was walking back home from a nearby shop in the village. In front of my home, I saw my neighbor and wished him. Suddenly he started talking to someone behind me. Then I turned to that side, and then no one was there. Suddenly I became blind while turning, the roadside bush touched my face, and I fell. Suddenly I opened my eyes, and I felt numbness all over my body.

My response: Okay, very nice. Glad to see you doing sadhan regularly. Kriyas are happening for you regularly. Please continue with your practice the same way. Please don't bother about the dream experiences. Kriyas are neither destroyed nor accumulated during the dream state.

Question: Same practitioner: It was not like an ordinary dream I had experienced earlier. The falling and touching feelings were actual and real.

My response: Okay. I understand that your dream was very intense. But nevertheless, please remember that karmas are neither created nor destroyed during the dream state. They are simply your sensual impressions accumulated in the subconscious mind surfacing when your mind is in the dream state. What happened after you woke up from your dream? It simply faded as a memory, although it appeared real while you were in the dream state. However, if you keep recollecting your dream, that memory will become fresh karma and might be repeated later. Please understand this. Therefore, just let it go. It doesn't mean anything else to you. It doesn't foretell any future events, either.

Question: A practitioner: I haven't been meditating regularly due to caring for my little baby. However, I do listen to my mantra using headphones at bedtime. Last night while listening to my mantra, I had a dream, and in it, I saw a cobra snake that was following me everywhere in my dream. Does that have to do with any kriya?

My response: The vision of a snake during a dream state is very auspicious for Shaktipat practitioners. Please don't worry about it. However, it is not deemed a kriya because karmas are neither created nor destroyed during the dream state. I am glad to know that you are listening to the mantra regularly. That amounts to the chanting of the mantra only. However, please don't start your sadhan till you recover fully after your recent childbirth.

Question: A practitioner: Today, during my afternoon nap, I dreamt of an unknown creature attacking me from behind. It was so heavy and started to bite me. Then, I started chanting Guru Mantra and pushed him back. Then, suddenly I came out of my dream.

My response: Okay. These kinds of strange dreams are usual after Shaktipat initiation. Please don't bother about them too much.

Question: A practitioner: My sadhan is going on in a usual fashion. Is sadhan connected with dreams also?

My response: Karmas are not destroyed or created during the dream state. However, dreams are experienced because of accumulated karma only.

Question: A practitioner: You said karmas are not destroyed during the dream state. Is that because karma is action and dreams are just meta-action?

My response: Yes, please, because we are only concerned with the consequences of our actions while we are in a waking state. Since those actions are tinged with egoism, they need to get eliminated while the mind is in the same state. During deep sleep, egoism is almost zero. Therefore, the sleep state also has no impact on our karma.

Question: A practitioner: I had a dream couple of days back that everyone in my house, in the dream, was dead on the same day. My mom, one of my distant grandmothers staying in our house years back, our domestic help, and a dog all died on the same day in my dream. I wanted to check if it signifies anything. Regarding my sadhan, I practice every Saturday and Sunday, lasting nearly an hour.

My response: Please don't worry about the dream at all. It doesn't signify anything at all. It is simply due to your accumulated karma in the past. Those karmas could be anything, including your fears and anxieties from past lives, which are mixed up and manifested now from your subconscious mind during the dream state. But please remember that karmas are neither destroyed nor freshly accumulated during the dream state.

Therefore, please do your sadhan regularly. During the waking state, only such karmas are destroyed while you are in sadhan. Why are you restricting your sadhan to only Saturday and Sunday, because you are giving a gap of 5 days in between? Sadhan done in that manner will not give you optimum benefit, although some karma will get destroyed. Sadhan should be regular. Daily or every alternate day, it should be like the oil pouring out from a vessel. In such a stream of sadhan, all your karmas are washed away speedily from your subconscious mind. Otherwise, I am happy to know that you are at least doing sadhan still.

Question: A practitioner: I dreamt of meeting my ex-girlfriend last night. We shared many good moments until her mother and sister entered the scene, and we even hugged each other. Then, her mother and sister (not real) came to create problems like in any other story, and the alarm rang, and I woke up. Is this related to kriya?

My response: No, please. During the dream state, karmas are neither destroyed nor accumulated. Hence, whatever happens during the dream state, is not kriyas. Although, they do give an indication of the karma accumulated in your subconscious mind. Please don't bother about it too much. If you keep on remembering your dream, then the memory of the dream will get accumulated as new karma. That is the idea.

Question: Same practitioner: So, does it mean that dreams do not convey any message which can change our lives? What is the real purpose of dreams, then? Is it just like the illusionary world in which we live?

Secrets of Shaktipat and Kundalini Yoga

My response: Accumulated karmas or sensual impressions surface in your subconscious. That is all about it. From the spiritual point of view, they don't impact your growth. Dreams don't have any impact on your life. They don't signify anything. A dream state is just a state of mind, although some people have tried to make art out of it. Dream interpretation is not even accepted by science as a precise science. As per the ancient yoga texts, they simply don't mean anything. Therefore, please don't get distracted by the dreams and just forget them. Yes, it is precisely like the illusionary world we live in.

Question: A practitioner: I sometimes get astonished by the dreams I see. A few days back, I saw myself becoming a Siddha, and many people gathered around me to seek a mantra to fulfill their earthly desires. Now I am convinced of the useless nature of dreams.

My response: They are probably your inner desires or accumulated karma. The desire to become a spiritual Guru is like any other materialistic desire. It is not different from other worldly desires in any way. Therefore, please don't focus your mind on such things. Please focus on your spiritual growth instead. Just bother about yourself only.

Question: A practitioner: I went to sleep last night; about half an hour into my sleep, I was woken up by a nightmare of my children drowning. And in the dream, I saved them from drowning. I was woken up and realized it was only a dream, and then I tried to go back to sleep.

Next, when I started to go back to sleep, I looked into my landscape. I saw a sea of fractal triangles covered in rainbow luminous light, filling my whole vision. My instant response was to think of my Guru. But the message that came through was that my Guru is already within the fractal triangles, within the light that I am observing, within me. It filled my whole vision, and I wasn't asleep. So, I left it and observed as I fell asleep.

My response: Strange dreams are usual for sadhaks because of the churning effect produced by the cosmic power within the subconscious mind. The second part must be Tandra state and not a dream. The upright triangle signifies Lord Shiva, and the inverted triangles inside signify Shakti or cosmic energy.

Question: A practitioner: Recently, my life has been very busy with hectic schedules and many domestic issues. I went to sleep early last night than on regular days at 11pm. Within a few minutes, I had a long dream with a vision of all of our Guru Mandali.

I was sitting opposite you. Beside you was Param Guru Swami Sahajanada Tirtha, and next to him was Swami Shivom Tirtha. Next to him was Swami Vishnu Tirtha, and next to him was Sri Yogananda. I could clearly see even Swami Narayan Dev Tirtha and Swami Gangadhar Tirtha. All were around me. I was observing all of our Gurus up to 3:30 am. It is the longest dream of my life. I am blessed with all Gurus' vision. But I am not able to understand the message.

My response: It's very auspicious to have the vision of your Guru during the dream state. Further, it is more auspicious to have the vision of all Gurus of our lineage. This shows your severe sadhan and how much your mind is focused on your Guru. Having the vision of Gurus of our lineage for such a prolonged time further indicates the seriousness of your sadhan. Please continue with your sadhan regularly in the same way.

Health-related issues

Question: A practitioner: Sharing my today's sadhan experience. I had a crushing sensation in my spleen and kidney area. It feels like a heavy pain. I had some sort of electric shock-like sensations in my stomach and head. I could not sit for more than 20 minutes; my mind was wandering. I was unable to focus.

Secrets of Shaktipat and Kundalini Yoga

My response: Okay, glad to see you doing sadhan. Please don't worry if you are not able to do sadhan for a long time. However, let's observe your kriyas more over the coming days. An electric shock-like sensation is understandable. But please be careful about the pain in the stomach and kidney areas. Please watch out for any health issues as well.

Question: A practitioner: Sharing my last night experiences in sadhan. I felt heavy vibrations all over my body. I felt some movements on the base of the spine. I had a vision of brilliant radiance. I experienced currents passing through the whole body. My neck and back felt very warm. There was a sudden pain in the stomach area. Heavy pain was felt inside my left ear, extending to my neck and head. At times felt wet in my inner left ear. I experienced mild physical kriyas. My head feels very heavy. I can now sit in Padmasana (lotus posture) for a long time without stretching my legs.

My response: Excellent that means asan is getting fructified for you now. You have started gaining posture stability. Please be careful about the stomach pain you have been experiencing for some time. Please don't shy away from checking out for any health issues. Other kriyas are normal only. No need to bother about them.

Question: A practitioner: Can I pray to our Gurus for relief from illness?

My response: Surely. But usually, Shaktipat is not known to be working for any materialistic benefits, as such. It is meant to burn down your karma. However, illness is also due to karma only. So, please understand this from that angle. If you are a regular sadhak, cosmic energy takes care of your worldly problems as a spin-off benefit. Otherwise, without regular sadhan, if someone wants to use Shaktipat for materialistic benefits, it will not work simply. Because you cannot fool God!

Question: A practitioner: Sorry to trouble you with this, but my brother-in-law has been diagnosed with an autoimmune disease called Gillian Barre. He is currently in hospital in Intensive care. Is there anything or prayers I can do for him remotely to assist in his healing?

My response: Oh! I am very sorry to hear about your brother-in-law's health condition. You can, of course, pray for him. If there is anyone who can do energy healing from a distance, like Reiki, etc., that can be tried on him. You can find some professionals online. Other than this, as a Shaktipat practitioner, you will not be able to influence his health because the benefit of awakened kundalini energy is strictly for your own self. It simply doesn't work in any other manner than cleaning up your karma. That is the issue here. I hope you understand it. I wish him a speedy recovery.

Question: A practitioner: I am suffering from a cold today. Can I practice sadhan during an infection?

My response: No, please. If you are not feeling physically or mentally well, please don't do sadhan. Please take a break. Get well soon.

Question: A practitioner: Last night, around 8:30-9 pm, I was walking around my house and felt pain in my skull. I was not doing any exercise or anything at that moment. I probably moved my head sideways, and it happened. The pain was constant as I moved my head.

Even while lying down to sleep, I could not lie down on my back but had to sleep sideways.

This morning I woke up and still had the pain. The sensation and pain are completely gone half an hour after waking up. I have never experienced anything like this. The pain was only in my skull, back of my head, and crown area, and the whole head felt heavy. Was this a kriya? I haven't done sadhan for the past 2-3 days as every time I do it, I have been feeling lethargic and depressed, so I was taking a break.

My response: Yes, please. It is a kriya only. Some of our sadhaks have also reported a similar type of kriyas, if not precisely the same. Please understand that kriya always goes on whether you are doing sadhan or not. However, we experience them pronouncedly when our minds are not engaged elsewhere. This means whenever the mind is in a contemplative mood, it is only deemed sadhan. Obviously, you will experience the kriyas.

Anyway, I am glad to see your progress. Please continue with your sadhan the same way regularly, and don't neglect the sadhan. At least keep your mind focused on your Guru during the day as much as possible, from when you wake up till you go off to sleep. This will offset the sadhan and will also benefit you greatly.

Hypersensitive mind

Question: A practitioner: Sharing my last night experiences in sadhan. All sorts of depressive thoughts appeared one after another. Even though it didn't bother me emotionally, the volume of thoughts did make me restless. I experienced subtler kriyas.

I felt currents on my neck, feet, and heart. I had a vision of brilliant radiance till the end. My back was very restless. My eyes felt very heavy. Pains felt in stomach and ribs. Then again, physical kriyas started off; with rotations, swinging left to right, back and forth, and neck moving in circles. I was very restless all 4 hrs in sadhan. Moreover, I feel to be by I all the time in solitude. I feel like going away from humans and joining some Ashram to lead a simple and pious life. Even traffic noise is too much for me now. Please Guide.

My response: Excellent; the mind becomes sensitive when a large chunk of karma is destroyed. But it is only a temporary phenomenon before it becomes immune to everything. I have discussed this phenomenon in my book, also. Please don't bother about it too much. Soon you may not feel it in the same way.

Similarly, Vairagya, or losing interest in the external world, starts developing. It seems it has started showing up for you. This is a very good phenomenon, but it needs to mature slowly and steadily. Please don't bother about joining any Ashram. It is not required because most people join Ashram to progress, so they don't get disturbed. In your case, sadhan is already happening without any obstruction. Therefore, it is not necessary for you at all.

Vishoka lights

Question: A practitioner: Question on this morning's sadhan; I started at 4.20 AM and finished just after 6:00 AM. At the end of the practice, I rubbed my eyes, and as I did so, I started to see blue and yellow electric light patterns. As I watched, it turned into a yellow eye with a tiny speck of yellow in the middle, like a small star. As I watched and focussed on the center, a swirling pattern appeared from that center back towards me, similar to a lighthouse projecting light. I removed my hands from my eyes, and the pattern remained as the physical kriyas moved through my body and spine. Is there any significance in seeing this, or is this another kriya?

My response: It is kriya only. Lights seen during sadhan are called Vishoka lights. They are subtle kriyas happening for cleaning your karmas only.

After death phenomenon

Question: A practitioner: As per the resources I have read, it says Shaktipat sadhan liberates you from the cycle of birth and death. But how does one know when it stops, and what does the soul do in the other astral plane after that?

My response: A vehicle or machine usually stops working under two conditions. Either due to mechanical breakdown or fuel exhaustion. A mechanical breakdown could be either due to a wear and tear accident or a sudden technical fault. In any case, a person knows that the machine has stopped working when it happens.

Either he goes for a new machine or gets it repaired if it's economically viable. However, if it's due to fuel exhaustion, the person knows it well in time and in real-time by reading the fuel gauge indicator. Either he gets it replenished constantly if the journey still needs to be completed or doesn't bother if the trip is about to be over before the fuel is exhausted.

Similarly, a human body stops functioning under two conditions; death or liberation. It is called death if the body becomes untenable to dwell for the soul due to general wear and tear/old age or accident or disease, both physically and mentally. It may opt for medical or psychological treatment if it's economically viable. In any case, it knows after it has quit the human body. It enters into a new womb to manufacture a new body for itself.

The second condition pertains to the exhaustion of the accumulated stock of karmas. That means it's karma that fuels life, whether in the human body or animal body. In this case, too, an awareness gets generated for the person as karma gets exhausted rapidly.

However, the indication is experienced from within. This is usually experienced in the form of bliss. Life also usually gets simplified. However, it's said that karma beneficial to society is experienced as it's about to get exhausted for a person. But the person has no choice but to dwell in the body because, technically, it's not feasible, just like one can't drive a vehicle if the fuel is exhausted.

I am saying this with one reservation. A few gentlemen had defied this law of karma. They must have lived on this planet without such fuel in the form of balance karma to propel their lives. I can't comment on those gentlemen. They are worshipped by mankind as Gods practicing various religions.

Keeping the above narrative in mind, I will try to answer the question of the sadhak. A soul knows it's liberated from the cycle of birth and death because it voluntarily quits the body. However, it's still tenable to dwell but technically not possible due to exhaustion of fuel/karma. From this point onwards, yoga is over as known to mankind. Because when karma gets exhausted mind comes to a standstill, and the person knows God.

Please recall the famous statement by Jesus from the Bible in this connection. God grandly proclaims, saying, "Still your mind and know that I am the God." This is the same statement in all yoga texts too. To still the mind is yoga. Hence, yoga known to mankind is over by attaining this objective of stillness of the mind.

After this, a new phase of spiritual ascension begins. Please remember that dualism is still retained at this stage. Awareness of self is still there even at this stage. Only the outermost sheath is gone when the gross human body is quit by the soul after exhaustion of all karma. The subtle body with remaining sheaths is still intact. However, it has no fuel/karma left to manufacture a new gross body of flesh and blood. Rather it would have quit the gross human body, although it's still tenable to dwell due to exhaustion of fuel/karma.

No one knows what happens after that. All yoga texts and various ancient Sanskrit texts have remained silent on this subject. No one has ever come back to tell the story because it is technically impossible to.

However, certain conclusions can be speculated based on ancient Sanskrit texts. I have tried to elaborate on this issue in my book The Illusion. Beings continue to exist in dualism after they cease to be human beings. Call them celestial beings or beings with subtle bodies. They retain the duality eternally. Some of them may be assuming heavenly bodies like stars and planets. They also keep getting disintegrated and are reborn again with each cycle of new universe creation. They keep practicing the final phase of the spiritual journey, called Shambhavopay, in Sanskrit.

In theory, the final merger with supreme cosmic power should get affected since there's only one divinity pervading the cosmos infinitely and eternally. But the timelines are too long for this final phase to get over if it ever happens. Hence, practically it is deemed that dualism exists eternally for the soul.

From this point of view, both the proponents of Advaita Vedanta, or monism, and Dvaita Vedanta, or dualism, are right in a way. We only end up in academic debates from this point onwards. My knowledge of these philosophies is zero. Hence, I can't answer the question posed by you as to what happens after getting liberated from the cycle of birth and death.

Contradictions in different books

Question: A practitioner: I have read in a book by Shivom Tirthji that the practice of kundalini should be performed only at night during Shukla Paksha. So, practicing in the morning of Krishna Paksha is not good?

My response: Ancient Yoga texts are meant for general guidance and that too for people practicing independent yoga systems like Ashtanga Yoga or Raja Yoga. Whereas you don't do any practice as such in our path other than sitting in a state of witness or silent spectator. The awakened kundalini energy does whatever has to be done inside your body and mind. So, where is the question of doing sadhan or practice here?

Hence, please understand it from this point of view. Since Swami Gangadhar Tirtha, all our Ashrams in India have been following this path of Shaktipat. They don't take any cognizance of any such teachings. Therefore, it does not apply to us. Please keep this in mind for your future reference also. You may find several contradictions on several platforms.

Books may say something, and YouTube or internet literature may say something. But all such literature pertains to independent yoga systems mainly. Even if it pertains to Shaktipat, it might differ from one parampara to another parampara. Whom do you believe? Which parampara is authentic? Which parampara is fake? Who is telling you the truth, and who is not? If you focus on other things, this is the problem.

There is nothing known as perfect sadhan or practice. Similarly, there is nothing known as a perfect yoga system. Just trust your Guru and have faith in the supreme cosmic power, not other things like books, etc. Please don't worry about these things. I am aware that you are only talking from the books of our parampara. If you see the above text in the picture, His Holiness only quoted certain sections of the ancient yoga texts. That is too generic, please.

In a way, we also follow the digits of the moon. This is why I don't give Shaktipat initiation on all days. But this is not applicable after Shaktipat initiation. All this is applicable before Shaktipat. Hence, please don't worry if you find something contradictory. Please don't focus on a thing in isolation.

Lastly, please don't mix up Vedic traditions with yoga traditions. For example, you are aware most of the Gurus in our parampara follow the sanyasa tradition by wearing saffron clothes, etc. However, His Holiness Sri Yogananda hasn't followed. Therefore, there is nothing sacrosanct in such things. What His Holiness was referring to in the above book is generally from a classical point of view as per ancient teachings.

Why all this discussion? My own Guru ji His Holiness Swami Sahajananda Tirtha (now 98 years old) has never talked about such restrictions for sadhan. He has been one of the direct disciples of His Holiness Swami Shivom Tirtha only at Dewas Ashram. Neither I saw this being followed in other Ashrams in India.

Issues related to day-dreaming

Question: A practitioner: During sadhan, I do day-dreaming. The flow of thoughts is natural and acceptable in sadhan. But, day-dreaming is like giving a forced direction to a random thought. Does it get classified as kriya? If not, what can be done about it? Because I notice that, in my case, most of the time during sadhan, it is consumed by these day-dreaming thoughts. I am confused about how sitting in sadhan makes it any different than sitting idle, which I do most of the time.

My response: There is a thin line between a natural thought arising in your mind and giving a forced direction to thought. The former is a kriya, and the latter will be new karma. But there is nothing to worry about because they are relatively easier to clear later. It is understandable that whenever a natural thought arises in your mind, it leads to a sequence of various thoughts. These sequences are also kriyas only in a way.

But please remember that if they are also naturally arising from the first thought, they are happening to clean up your karma. But suppose you deliberately try to think about something to clean up your karma about that subject. In that case, it will become a new karma.

Just remember the thumb rule that you can't fool the all-knowing cosmic energy. As long as you don't intend to deceive the cosmic energy, there is nothing to worry about. Sometimes practitioners get too passionate about their thoughts. Please don't worry about it too much. They are relatively easier to clear later, even if they happen to get accumulated as karma. But please don't try to fool the supreme cosmic power. That is all that you need to understand. Giving forced direction to a thought needs to be understood from the above perspective. I hope you are clear now.

Question: Same practitioner: It is pretty clear, but the problem is the mind is difficult to control. Intellectually we can understand the above concept, but in action, it is challenging to understand what is going on in one's mind. We can only pray to you and Guru Parampara for help.

My response: Yes, I agree with you. That is why I said there is a fragile line between karma and a kriya. It is difficult to figure out when a natural thought slips into a passionate thought, or you give it a forced direction. But there is no need to worry about it. Even if it accumulates as new karma, it is relatively easier to clear later. Therefore, there is no need to bother about it. Please understand that the more subtle a kriya, the more it becomes prone to accumulate as new karma. In fact, there are other types of kriyas related to the erosion of egoism that is more difficult to understand.

For example, a practitioner undergoes some kind of public humiliation as part of the kriyas. In such a case, the unpleasant experience is more likely to accumulate as karma. Understandably, practitioners may be unable to exercise adequate dispassion while undergoing such experiences. But there is nothing to worry about it too much. As I have repeatedly said, such fresh karma is cleaned up easily later. Please apply this thumb rule to various thoughts and emotions arising during sadhan. Just don't bother about them. Be brave and continue with your practice during such moments.

Timelines for fructification of Mahayoga

Question: A practitioner: I have heard that it had taken more than one life for many sages to attain liberation. Even in some cases, if a person has been given Shaktipat initiation by their Guru in their past lives, the same person, when he or she is reborn, will not know anything about their past life. They are likely to commit many sins before being initiated by

Secrets of Shaktipat and Kundalini Yoga

the Guru. So, the person has to suffer the karma of that life, too, right? Why doesn't the divine make all this happen in a single life? So, that the person is at least spared of the karma of his / her future life/lives?

My response: Yes, what you heard is correct. After Shaktipat, it usually takes more than one life to attain the state of Samadhi, or a thoughtless state. But I repeat again only to reach the state of Samadhi and not moksha. However, it is also said that the mahayoga can get fructified in 6 or 9, or 12 years depending on the seriousness of the sadhan. But these are broad yardsticks. Mostly it is all academic stuff. On a serious note, predicting the results and timelines is impossible.

The reason for this is the enormous volumes of karma accumulated by the practitioner from past lives. However, a practitioner begins the journey in the next life precisely from where he left it. That is the silver lining. However, a practitioner commits more and more karma in the meantime. It is a continuous process. You can't do it neat and clean. That is simply not possible.

It is akin to repairing a road while the traffic is on. The problem is not caused by God but by the practitioner himself or herself. It is all related to the balance account of karmas. From a yoga point of view, it is possible to reach the state of Samadhi in one life also. Lastly, you are again using the word "sins." Please understand that yoga doesn't differentiate between saints and sinners. Therefore, please use the word "karma" always and everywhere.

Intellectual amusement

Question: A practitioner: Please elaborate on intellectual amusement. If we read or see Ramayana and become emotional, does it also make fresh karma?

My response: Anything you enjoy through the physical senses is called body amusement. Anything you want through the mind is called emotional amusement. Anything you enjoy through the intellect is called intellectual amusement. This could be in two parts; one pertains to arts like literature, music, philosophy, etc. the other to sciences like; logical deduction, rational thinking, etc.

In a nutshell, all that pertains to creativity. In the case of actions like reading scriptures like Ramayana or watching it in drama form etc., getting emotional is obviously related to emotional amusement. This emotional amusement is broadly divided into nine categories; humor, romance, compassion, disgust, etc. Obviously, if your mind is engaged in any of these emotions, that becomes emotional amusement. However, scriptures like Ramayana also deal with intellectual entertainment because a lot of discussion about ethics is also found in them. Therefore, it depends upon who is reading it. If an intelligent person reads it, they may discover intellectual amusement.

Since your above question is pointed at the emotional side of it, obviously, it is deemed to be for emotional amusement. Lastly, please understand one crucial issue so that you don't get confused or overwhelmed by anything, however grand it may appear. Anything pertaining to body, mind, or intellect is all within the realm of the Maya, illusion, or cosmic energy. SELF is supposed to be even beyond the realm of this cosmic energy. But then, yoga is not concerned with the SELF since its jurisdiction is only to make the mind reach a thoughtless state.

Religion and spirituality

Question: A practitioner: Why don't we treat Religion and Spirituality as the paths for a holy living in their proper perspective?

My response: People who practice independent yoga systems like the path of devotion or Bhakti Yoga do that, but it does not apply to Shaktipat practitioners. Whatever people aim to achieve in independent yoga systems is already attained

Secrets of Shaktipat and Kundalini Yoga

simply by the grace of the Guru after Shaktipat. Being religious and pious is only a technique applied in Bhakti Yoga. It is just a means to trick the mind into samadhi.

In fact, there are several other yoga systems and tantric methods for attaining spiritual growth. Therefore, why will everyone treat religion and piety as the only means to pursue spirituality? Please understand this from this perspective.

Lastly, please remember that you don't return to high school after graduating. Being religious and pious, even after Shaktipat, amounts to the same thing. Unfortunately, people get scared to stop practicing religion. As a result, religion becomes an obstacle to yoga practitioners after Shaktipat. I don't mean to say that everyone should stop practicing religion immediately because everyone may not have the required mental conditions. However, one should refrain from holding on to religion stubbornly after Shaktipat. I hope you got a general idea now.

Sex related issues

Question: A practitioner: Is sex a natural thing, like food and sleep, in everybody? Or does it create its own karma?

My response: Five organs of action in the human body perform five different types of karmas. Procreation is one such karma by which God's propagation of the species is done. That is why the genital organ has been designed for the human body. But it is not mandatory karma like eating and sleeping.

That means a human doesn't need to help God in the propagation of the species. If he tries to do that, he or she is obviously caught in the divine play of God known as Maya or the cosmic illusion.

Whereas eating food is mandatory karma for maintaining the body, so yoga can be performed in the initial stages. In advanced stages, the requirement of performing these karmas may not be there. There is something known as the stream of ambrosia which is supposed to get secreted into the throat from the upper portion. The practitioner's body is supposed to be nourished and sustained till moksha is obtained. This is obviously to spare the practitioner from accumulating new karma related to maintaining the body.

Secrets of Shaktipat and Kundalini Yoga

From this perspective, indulging in sexual activity amounts to fulfilling carnal desires. These result in the accumulation of new karma. It is akin to eating food over and above the basic requirements. For example, eating pizza may not be mandatory for the sustenance of the body. However, it helps fulfill the carnal desires pertaining to taste. Therefore, all five organs of action are interlinked with the five sensory organs helping accumulate karmas.

Lastly, it is an indiscriminate indulgence that creates enormous volumes of new karma. Minimal indulgence will also accumulate karmas, but they will be relatively easy to clear later. Please try and understand this entire concept comprehensively and not in isolation. Otherwise, there is a danger of misunderstanding my message.

People indulge in fulfilling their carnal desire under the excuse that it is a natural thing to do. What is the crux of the reason for indulgence? That counts. A practitioner needs to be truthful to him or herself. Then the answer is revealed internally. However, practitioners need not get scared too much on this count. What I have said above is applicable in a perfect scenario of yoga practice.

Otherwise, indulgence in sensual pleasures, knowing that they will add up to karmas, does take place with almost every practitioner in the initial stages. Slowly the interest is lost. That is called "vairagya," or losing interest in the external world. Therefore, there is no definite rule on whether sex is sinful or natural. It depends upon the situation. Definitely, it creates new karma. That is the bottom line.

People practicing independent yoga systems like Ashtanga Yoga avoid it so that it helps them conserve something known as "Ojas." In our path, such necessity is not there. Please don't bother about all this academic stuff. Just focus your mind on sadhan. All the answers are revealed to you internally as you progress on the path of yoga. Otherwise, there is a danger of drifting away from the main course and getting into intellectual amusement of the mind. Intellectual amusement is also like any other fulfillment of carnal desires.

Question: A practitioner: I am doing better today than yesterday. I did some pranayama too. I just want to ask you whether, due to the awakening of kundalini, one loses interest in sex. I am really losing interest now.

My response: There is nothing like that in the initial stages. Instead, it increases sometimes due to the movement of energy near the Svadhisthana Chakra, which happens as a kriya. A general loss of interest in the materialistic world, which is called vairagya, will start. But it occurs at much later stages, covering all aspects of life and not sex only in isolation. But suppose it is happening to you in isolation regarding the sexual urge. In that case, it is only a temporary phenomenon.

Please don't bother or focus your mind too much on thinking that you lost interest in sex. Remember that your body will not be affected adversely after the kundalini energy awakening. This includes the sex organ. It may happen only during accidental awakening without formal supervision from a Guru. Otherwise, no need to worry about it at all. However, please check out for other health issues, like mental stress, etc.

Question: A practitioner: My experiences from the past 3-4 weeks. I have been having a lot of vibrations in the back of my spine near Svadisthana Chakra and Heart Chakra. I am having severe nasal congestion, especially at 3:30 am. I wake up breathless. I feel third-eye vibrations sometimes.

My response: It is observed that after awakening kundalini energy in a person, nasal congestion occurs, usually in the aftermath of an intense sexual act. You said that vibrations are occurring in Svadhisthan Chakra. The close proximity of the genital organ to the Svadhisthan Chakra could result in nasal congestion. Ida and Pingala nadis which originate from Muladhara Chakra, terminate in the nostrils on opposite sides. That means ida nadi starts from the left side, ends in the right nostril, and vice versa. As I understand, this could be the reason for the nasal congestion. It is kriya only. Hence no need to bother about it at all.

Question: A practitioner: What should women do with sexual energy? Is masturbation a waste of life force? Should women build this energy by retaining it? If a woman is single with nobody to have loving sex with, what is the best thing to do?

Reply by another practitioner: As per my discussion with Guru Ji, these questions and the psychology behind them will get resolved automatically as you progress in the meditation. So, leave it to the divine force to do as it pleases. This path makes you a passenger on autopilot. Your job is to pay respects to the Guru parampara and meditate as instructed by the Guru. All these psychological knots that we tie ourselves to will automatically get resolved by the grace of our Gurus and your sadhan. This is what I have understood.

My response: Please understand that the issue raised by you pertains not only to women but also to men. However, retaining sex energy by abstaining from sexual activity both physically and mentally does not apply to all yoga practitioners. Celibacy is recommended to be practiced mainly in Ashtanga Yoga or Raja Yoga for awakening kundalini energy.

It is said that sex energy, when retained, is converted into something known as "Ojas." As per the yoga texts, the impact a person has over their fellow humans is supposed to be dictated by the power of "Ojas" only. Retaining sex energy is also considered to be good for the bones and joints, as per modern science. I remember reading about it somewhere, although my knowledge of contemporary science is zero.

Otherwise, in various other yoga systems, celibacy is not practiced. In fact, in certain tantric techniques, it is a mandatory requirement also. What a single person or married person should do has nothing to do with yoga practice. Any action, when performed indiscriminately, is karma only. Why talk about sex? There are other mandatory karmas as well like; eating or bathing or wearing clothes etc. If a person is excessively addicted to such things, obviously, he or she will be accumulating karma.

Therefore, there is no prescribed rule for the questions raised by you. In our path abstaining from sexual activity is not mandatory since the purpose has already been served by the grace of the Guru.

What should a single woman do when she has no husband to have sex with is a social issue. It has nothing to do with yoga practice. But please remember that any action undertaken to fulfill sensual pleasures becomes karma. How a person should overcome the emotion of sex is like any other issue.

Some people have extreme tempers or other emotional problems. If you do your yoga practice regularly, all such issues get resolved internally as your karmas are eliminated. It does not mean that a person loses interest in sex or the sex organ becomes defunct. But he or she will be able to keep it in check perfectly.

Definitely, someone is not going to die for not engaging in sex. It may be a biological phenomenon but not a mandatory one like eating food. I hope your doubts are cleared to some extent by the above explanation. It is not such a big deal to bother about. Also, there is nothing known as any perfect thing to do. Yoga is all about how you manage to free yourself from your karma.

Question: Same practitioner: The reason I specifically asked about women was that I have wondered if the benefit of retaining was for men only. Also, if the energy could be used in ways other than just releasing it and creating karma. You mentioned 'Ojas,' so the sexual energy can be used to have power over other humans? I will look it up, as I am interested in different perspectives on sexual energy. It must be more important or valuable than just releasing mindlessly. I have heard of tantra also. Although I don't have much knowledge, and I assume it is used in combination with the energy of the opposite sex, I could be wrong.

My response: You can Google and learn more about the "Ozas" or "Ojas," just watch out for the spelling in English. But it does not apply to practitioners of Shaktipat. Please remember that our path is akin to a college and various independent yoga systems are akin to high schools. Obviously, you don't go back after your graduation.

Question: Another practitioner: So, karma from releasing sexual energy is no different from the karma accumulated when eating food? So, depending on how or why the action is taken would determine what type of karma it would create? So, suppose you are releasing this energy. In that case, are you not losing power or inhibiting the kundalini from rising in any way? I understand now that, as you say, it has been used to awaken the kundalini in some yoga practices. It is, however, not needed in our path. But once it is awakened, does this energy not have any use other than to create karma?

My response: No, please. Because after awakening, the kundalini energy is in reverse mode. This is a destructive mode, whereas sex energy is basically creative energy. Creative energy creates "Maya," or the cosmic illusion. They are in opposite directions, although the energy is always the same. That means energy is indivisible. Please, don't waste your time trying to study and experiment with all these things at this stage. You are already at an advanced level after Shaktipat initiation. You might get distracted. Please be careful about this. It is better to focus your mind sharply on your sadhan or practice.

Question: A practitioner: I have to ask something private. Is it okay to masturbate?

I asked the question because I see so many videos; even Sadguru said you should not waste your fluid. But Buddha said, Madhya Marg. One can do it sometimes. Not too much and not too less. Krishna Murari said masturbation will lower your energy.

My response: If it is happening in sadhan or you feel a strong urge for that, it is a kriya. Otherwise, if you deliberately do it, then it is karma you are creating. Also, our path has no restrictions on lifestyle, eating habits, sex, etc. Although, it will all fade away at a very later stage as you advance in your sadhan. All those ideas of different Gurus are not meant for practitioners of Shaktipat. They are preparing practitioners for the awakening of the kundalini.

In our case, kundalini is awakened directly by the grace of our Lineage. Gurus and Divine Mother know what is for our highest good. She has control over everything now. So, the question of wastage of power, energy, semen, etc., does not arise. Also, so much literature and videos are available online. If you watch all those, you will be confused, resulting in an obstacle to your sadhan. Because they are way off from our Shaktipat.

Question: A practitioner: I would like to ask about the issue of sexual desire. A short time ago, I realized that this is no longer a focus of my mind or body. I am enjoying other activities, mainly spiritual issues. Why is this happening?

My response: Sex desires are akin to any other sensual desires. They are fuelled by accumulated karma within. As a sadhak progresses by burning down of karmas, he starts losing interest in worldly things. That means they aren't as important to him anymore as they used to be earlier. However, there's no need to worry about it. A few sadhaks expressed their apprehension that their sex organ may become defunct. Health will not get affected adversely. Sex organs will also not get affected adversely. It's just that they may start losing interest in sexual activity. It's too early to say whether this can be called vairagya (comprehensive loss of interest in the external world) or not in your case. The outbound creative energy projected into the outer world has now started retracting. However, much more needs to happen further. You need to lose interest in many other things pertaining to various other desires, both physical, mental, and intellectual. As karmas related to multiple categories start getting cleaned up, these flames of desires raging in an outbound direction start retracting. This is called vairagya. Hence, it can be said that it's the beginning of vairagya for you. However, it needs to get more and more mature.

Question: A practitioner: Today's sadhan is too different. Pardon me, Guru Ji, but because of sexual feelings, too much fluid has come out.

My response: Excellent. That is okay. Very normal. But please don't resist the kriyas. Let the thoughts come into your mind. Let the fluid also come out.

Kundalini energy related issues

General doubts

Question: A practitioner: Does kundalini, once awakened, goes into sleeping mode again? If a person has various bad karmas, does the kundalini show slow effects?

My response: Once kundalini energy is awakened, it remains active till moksha is attained. It is carried forward to the next life. That is why we have some practitioners in whom kundalini energy was already active before I gave Shaktipat deeksha to them. Please remember that Shaktipat deeksha has to be compulsorily taken in every birth formally under a Guru, although kundalini energy is already active. This is a mandatory phenomenon.

It is akin to a person undergoing schooling every time afresh in every lifetime, although that person was highly educated in their previous life. That means he must have had those memories embedded in the subconscious mind, but still, he needs to undergo formal schooling. The same applies to kundalini energy also.

Next, your bad or negative karmas don't slow down the kundalini energy. Kundalini energy doesn't differentiate between good karma and bad karma. The words good and

Secrets of Shaktipat and Kundalini Yoga

bad exist only in the human dictionary. I am surprised that you have asked me these questions. It seems you have not read my book thoroughly. I have also answered similar questions repeatedly earlier. Therefore, I request you to kindly read the books shared with you. Otherwise, it takes unnecessary additional work to answer the same question repeatedly. I hope you understand my problem also.

Question: Same practitioner: No, sir, I already read your books. Sorry to ask you again. Recently I read a book in Marathi related to kundalini. In that book, I read the article that if you don't follow the rules of kundalini and if you eat onion and garlic, kundalini goes into sleeping mode. This will harm health also; that is why I needed clarification.

My response: What can I say about something you read from somewhere? The proper method of obtaining knowledge is always from your Guru and not from other sources. Otherwise, it amounts to self-treatment, and you are aware of the dangers involved in self-treatment. Anyone can Google around and find out what medicine to take before going and purchasing it from a medical shop. But is it the proper way? The same thing applies to spiritual sciences also.

You must follow the proper method to obtain knowledge. Otherwise, what is the requirement of a Guru? You can rely on books and the internet only. Please understand that your urge to explore on your own will confuse you and force you out of the main path of yoga. That is why it is suggested that practitioners don't bother about anything else other than their Guru.

If I have to answer why it was written that way in the book you read, it is impossible for me to read all such stuff on the internet. Moreover, a lot of literature on the internet regarding kundalini energy awakening mostly belongs to independent yoga systems like; Ashtanga Yoga or Raja Yoga. They abstain from non-vegetarian foods, alcohol, pungent and bitter foods, etc., to prepare their minds for awakening kundalini energy. They may continue with the same habits even after awakening kundalini energy.

In our path, you don't have to follow any rules regarding food habits or drinking habits. I have explained this to you before giving you Shaktipat deeksha. You are mixing up our Shaktipat with other independent yoga systems. All that you have read does not apply to us. I also want to refrain from commenting on the authenticity of the book you read and its author.

Therefore, many questions will arise, leading to confusion if you drift away from the main path. Lastly, have you read the compiled questions and answers book shared with all? I remember answering this on a few occasions earlier, also. I request you to kindly read it; if not, read it. I have made most of the basics clear to everyone in both books.

To my knowledge, onion and garlic have excellent medicinal value. People following Ashtanga Yoga avoid it so that it helps them in controlling their minds by developing satvic guna. Similarly, people who worship Vishnu also avoid it, so satvic guna is developed. That is all about it. It has nothing to do with kundalini energy awakening.

Kundalini is awakened only when there is equilibrium in the three gunas; rajo guna, tamo guna, and satva guna. Onion and garlic must promote rajo guna or tamo guna; therefore, avoiding them is for something else and not directly related to kundalini energy awakening. It is akin to high school knowledge, whereas you are now in college after Shaktipat initiation. Please don't burden yourself with all that knowledge that is no longer required.

Question: A practitioner: Why is meditation given so much importance? Why should we focus our attention on our breath? Why can a person reach the stage of samadhi only through meditation?

Secrets of Shaktipat and Kundalini Yoga

Only by practicing meditation is Kundalini Shakti able to cross all the Chakras. Why is there no other method (Apart from Shaktipat)?

Why is Kundalini Shakti in a dormant state in every person?

How would his life be if a person were born with his Kundalini Shakti active? How do we recognize them, Guru Ji?

My response: I request you to please read my book once again. All of your above questions have been adequately addressed in the book. It seems you have not read the book thoroughly. That could be the reason why you are asking the above questions. They are too basic questions which you asked above. Obviously, it will take a lot of time trying to answer them.

Meditation is simply one of the techniques used to trick the mind into a state of thoughtlessness or samadhi. Samadhi is the end aim of all yoga or tantric systems. It is more popular because of the materialistic benefits associated with meditation. Obviously, one of the main reasons is to gain supernatural powers. People get attracted to meditation because of this, although they can get the same from other paths. However, the benefits start manifesting quickly during meditation compared to other paths. Even a little bit of meditation brings in a lot of benefits from a materialistic point of view. Hence, people tend to get attracted more to this path.

People are required to focus on breathing to gain control over the life force operating within the body. However, this is also one of the techniques used to awaken kundalini energy. Further, it is part of Hatha Yoga. That means you don't find everyone who practices meditation focussing their attention on breathing only. It depends upon the technique being used.

There are various other methods by which kundalini is made to ascend along the cerebral spinal system. You may not be aware of them. However, kundalini energy is called by different names in different systems. That is why I said that you need to read my book properly. You need to understand the concept broadly and comprehensively first. Otherwise, you tend to get carried away by the literature you find in books and on the internet. You tend to focus on each technique in isolation without realizing that it is only one among many other methods used to awaken kundalini energy.

Kundalini energy remains at the bottom of the spinal system and continuously projects the illusionary world on the psyche of the human being. For ease of understanding, it is referred to as being in a sleep state. Otherwise, the all-knowing and conscious cosmic energy is eternally awake.

Lastly, there are many sadhaks among you all who already had kundalini energy in the awakened state in their bodies before receiving Shaktipat deeksha from me. They are like you only. Their life also unfolds for them as per their accumulated karma, just like yours. In this connection, please understand that everyone has to formally take Shaktipat deeksha in every human birth until they obtain moksha. A Shaktipat Guru's concern is to recognize such persons based on kriyas manifesting for them. Therefore, please don't bother about such knowledge. You can read my books on Q & A. Some sadhaks have revealed their kriyas before and after Shaktipat deeksha.

Question: A practitioner: How to know the location of our kundalini shakti? I mean, where my kundalini is now. Is that in the Muladhara chakra or in another chakra? Sorry if I asked any wrong or unnecessary questions.

My response: The question does not apply to our path. It is applicable more to independent yoga systems like Ashtanga yoga or Raja yoga. In such independent yoga systems, kundalini energy is awakened from one chakra to the next,

Secrets of Shaktipat and Kundalini Yoga

step by step. Obviously, practitioners undergo all kinds of experiences pertaining to each chakra. That is why the question arises as to till which level the kundalini energy has been awakened in a person. But all that literature pertains to initial levels.

It is akin to high school knowledge or traveling in a passenger train when you realize all the intermediate minor stations en route. Whereas our path is at a much higher level. It is akin to a college or traveling on an express train. You don't come to know the minor stations en route. After Shakthipat initiation, kundalini energy is awakened in an individual comprehensively. The entire cerebrospinal system gets activated. As a result, the burning down of karma starts.

When this process of burning down of karmas is going on, its impact is felt on various chakras as kriyas. When someone experiences kriya in a particular chakra, it can be said that kundalini energy is active in that chakra in loose terms. But it does not mean that kundalini is active only in that particular chakra. Later kriya might happen in a lower chakra. Then the practitioner might get confused about why kundalini is going down instead of going up. It is a wrong understanding.

Otherwise, kundalini energy is already awakened and activated comprehensively after Shakthipat. All karmas are related to one chakra or the other in the cerebrospinal system. For example, suppose kriyas related to smell are taking place. In that case, the root chakra is activated because it is associated with the sensory organ of smell. Similarly, others!

Therefore, the above question doesn't pertain to our path. All practitioners should read the compiled questions and answers first. Many such questions have already been answered earlier. Otherwise, it is getting repetitive, please. I request all practitioners to kindly read the book pdfs first. If any other doubt is left, you are most welcome to ask me.

Question: A practitioner: Can this force, after initiation, influence other people and life events?

Colonel T Sreenivasulu

This is why I ask: since the initiation, I do sadhan daily, experiencing no sensations in my psyche or bodily manifestation, but I have noticed other things outside myself. One week after initiation, I noticed my wife and my son started exhibiting newly visible positive strength. My wife is noticeably motivated. She got a new job at the local school (she moved to Germany a year ago, and she is a teacher) and obtained her license to teach from the German government, which actually takes 2 to 3 years because we are not from the European Union. It is too difficult with a work visa, diploma acceptance, etc.

After initiation, my wife got a work visa and a job at the school quickly, like we had never heard of. My son is able to overcome difficulties in new culture, land, and language very quickly, all strongly noticeable now after initiation.

I had an accident last week, and I have recovered in 3 days without scars or pain. I have noticed that many usually difficult things are now easy for me. Also, people who communicate with me are more optimistic, motivated, and joyous. I could not deny that all of this that happened so unusually is connected with this force that is moved through initiation. Am I correct in this thought!!?

I experienced new mental strength and overcame obstructions much easier than before.

I look at the situation and conclude that this has had an effect since initiation.

Accidental awakening

Question: A practitioner: I got home from work, went through the Shaktipat lineage, and tried to learn all the names of the Gurus. I watched your videos and made my desktop screensaver your image. Is it possible to get initiated accidentally by absorbing all this before the Shaktipat deeksha?

Secrets of Shaktipat and Kundalini Yoga

I started having a silent dialogue with the Swamis and then focused on your image. I focused on your image to have it in mind for the deeksha time on Sunday. I was directed to go within and sit in meditation with your image. I don't know why but I did it. After all that, I became still and felt the kundalini energy. I first felt pressure in my head and then some movements in my spine. I left the meditation to write you. Is this normal?

The more I focused on your image, the more intense it became. This is definitely for real. I knew I would have difficulty remembering every name except a few. So, I went to each of them and asked them to help me on the inner planes during my initiation. I kept seeing your picture in my third eye and repeated your name. That is when I was guided to sit and felt this.

Again, the more I focused on your image, the more intense it became. I felt the kundalini energy at my base. I felt pressure in my skull. Then, I started to feel vibrations around my spine. I remembered the book saying to go with it, so I did. I left the meditation to check with you about this. As my Guru Ji, I thought you should know about this experience.

My response: Yes, some practitioners have been reporting that after reading the book, they have started experiencing kriyas. That is okay. Our group has some practitioners who already had their kundalini energy awakened. This must have been the carry forward from their previous lives.

However, Shaktipat initiation in a formal manner is mandatory in every lifetime till self-realization is attained. Shaktipat is done for two reasons; to awaken kundalini energy and to stabilize the already awakened energy. In this case, it must have been a combination of carrying forward from your previous life and the impact of reading the book. The book reading must have resulted in the ideal conditions set in your mind.

Activation of chakras after Shaktipat

Colonel T Sreenivasulu

Question: A practitioner: I have been in a meditation zone with solid energy since night and morning. Can you please explain if all my Chakras are activated? If they are activated, the next step is to attain moksha because these thoughts are coming rapidly to my mind, so I can't control myself from asking you. Once it is clear, I can calmly do sadhan again.

My response: All your Chakras and the entire cerebrospinal system are activated comprehensively by Shaktipat deeksha. We don't even use the phrase Chakra activation because that kind of thing is done in independent yoga systems. That is like high school knowledge. You are now in college after Shaktipat.

Therefore, there is nothing known as Chakra activation in our path. It is deemed to have been activated comprehensively. Rather it is all about the burning down of karma. Please don't try and compare our path with the literature available on the internet about independent yoga systems. This could be why you have so many doubts about ideas like; Chakra activation or connecting with the soul or guidance from the soul etc. That is all applicable in the preliminary stages.

You are most welcome to ask me any number of questions, but please read the book of compiled questions and answers first. Most of your doubts will get cleared. I remember explaining these things on several occasions earlier also. Unfortunately, sadhaks are not reading those books.

Questions are asked repeatedly again and again on the same subject. Trying to explain the same thing is a waste of time and effort. I hope you understand my problem also. Otherwise, you can always ask me se, if you don't find answers.

As to the second part of the question: You can't calmly practice sadhan, please. That calmness you seek will come at later stages after your karmas start getting neutralized, not before that. Sadhan is all about burning down karmas. A calm mind is the effect of it, or it is the result of sadhan. For example, you study hard so that you pass your exams. You can't say that pass me in the exam first so that I can study without any anxiety.

Question: A practitioner: I feel the warmth/heat of the energy in my Muladhara when I do sadhan. I also start to feel the vibrations at the Ajna Chakra. Will there be energy awakened in the other Chakras too? If yes, why I do not feel the same in the other Chakras?

My response: When traveling in an Express train, you don't notice small rail stations en route. But definitely, the train passes through all stations. However, when you travel in a passenger train, you stop at every tiny station. Similarly, Shaktipat is like traveling on an Express train. Please don't compare this with other literature you must have read; about independent Yoga systems like Ashtanga Yoga or Raja Yoga. They are like passenger trains.

Therefore, all experiences encountered by a person in independent yoga systems are not experienced by a Shaktipat practitioner. Please focus your mind on your Guru and the mantra. That is all you must do. Otherwise, your progress will be slow if you keep getting distracted by your knowledge of the subject read in books or on the internet. Instead, trust your Guru and the Shaktipat.

Sadhan

Slipping down during sadhan

Question: A practitioner: (On slipping down during sadhan) I have read in your book that some people have rapid spiritual development and may also fall down from that development. Can you please explain how?

My response: It is not because of any rapid development as such. It usually happens with everyone. Slipping down from the progress achieved is a very common problem faced by almost every yoga practitioner. It is a natural phenomenon. Common reasons are; not being regular in practice, not exercising adequate self-surrender to the divinity, or getting attracted to worldly activities. The higher a practitioner reaches on the path of yoga, the more slippery it is. Although there is nothing to worry about, one just needs to be careful.

Question: A practitioner: In your book, it is mentioned that relapse can happen to practitioners. How can a sadhak realize it and avoid it? What are the necessary precautions to be taken to avoid it?

My response: The path of yoga is very slippery in nature. The more you reach, the higher levels, and the more slippery it is. A sadhak can quickly realize this when he observes the difference in his or her state of mind. It is a very normal phenomenon. It happens to almost everyone. The remedy is to start over again. Start doing sadhan again. Start climbing up once again. However, if a practitioner is regular in sadhan, there is no fear of significant slippery. All said and done, it is very normal. Just nothing to bother about it!

Sadhan timings

Question: A practitioner: I am very happy and encouraged to keep going. I have been doing my practice before bed. I suppose one can do it as often as we need to?

My response: Yes, please. You can do it as often as you wish and for as much time as possible. Please remember to always keep your mind focused on your Guru and the mantra. Whatever happens to you is only through the medium of your Guru and the mantra. Please don't entertain the idea of I'ness or egoism while doing sadhan or practice. Just surrender yourself completely but sincerely from the bottom of your heart.

Focussing mind on Guru during sadhan

Question: A practitioner: I am sharing my experiences of the past few days. You answered a query by a fellow sadhak, saying that the devotee should only focus on his Guru. From that day on, I started focusing on you. Then one day, I suddenly witnessed that you were there in my entire body, and I was experiencing a lot of kriyas.

After some time, one day, I saw that my body, which had you in it, had become so big that, gradually, it filled every corner of the sky.

Meanwhile, there were various kinds of movements in my spine, sometimes, the movements were like a snake's movement, and at other times they were like half-sine waves. My head went back as if it would touch my back. I felt my neck would break.

I often see a blue light in my third eye, Chakra, but that isn't permanent.

Then three days ago, during the night, kriyas started off, where I felt someone had kept ice on my head, and my entire head became very cold.

The kriyas go on for 24 hours; I can feel them, and sometimes they become very intense. I offer my salutations repeatedly to your lotus feet.

My response: Excellent, I am very happy for you. I wish you had done the same thing from the beginning. Anyway, it is better late than never. At last, kriyas have begun for you, and that too full-blown. Glad to know the news. Just continue with your sadhan the same way henceforth.

All practitioners are requested to make a special note of the above experience. This is the mistake that many practitioners make. Please follow the correct way of practicing sincerely from the bottom of your heart. In a nutshell, just do what you are supposed to do with complete self-surrender to the divinity.

Question: Same practitioner: Please enlighten me, Guru Ji, is what's going on at night also normal?

My response: Yes, please. They are also kriyas only. Everything will get sorted out as the sensual impressions accumulated in your subconscious mind or the karmas get cleaned up. Please understand that whatever you are experiencing is nothing but your own internal world. The remedy is to burn it down. But you can't do this with your own efforts.

The awakened kundalini energy does it in autonomous mode. You need to allow the supreme cosmic power or the awakened kundalini energy to do its job without resisting. It will also take time. Therefore, just surrender yourself completely to the divinity or Guru. Keep your mind focused on your Guru as much time as possible. Day and night. Simultaneously please keep repeating the mantra given to you. Rapidly your karma will start getting drained out of your system. You are the eternal spirit. Pure and limitless. Therefore, please be brave.

Obstacles during sadhan

Question: A practitioner: After today's sadhan, I had a strong urge to sleep. It was so strong that my eyes were closing without my control. As if I didn't have the strength to stay awake. Was it a kriya? Or a symptom of normal sleep. Because I usually don't feel sleepy after sadhan in the morning. So, I resisted and didn't sleep because I had to go out to work.

My response: Actually, it is a kriya only. More so as an obstacle in your sadhan! That means some negative karma accumulated by you in the past about yoga practice is now being cleaned. In the past, you may have criticized the yoga systems or shown some kind of negative attitude towards yoga practice. Those negative karmas are catching up when you are seriously into this field. But it happens with many practitioners. Nothing to worry about it at all! Soon those negative karmas will also get exhausted. Just keep doing sadhan with persistence.

Mental conditions during sadhan

Question: A practitioner: Is it lethargy, anxiety, or what else? I am not able to figure it out. I sit for sadhan, but I cannot sit for long periods. Sometimes, thoughts cause me so much anxiety that I immediately get up and get into action. The weird fact is that I get up to do things to be done in the afternoon, like taking a position in the share market.

Sometimes, I feel so lethargic that I want to go and sleep while doing sadhan. I get up and don't even go to bed. Sometimes, I just want to get up for no reason. I started sitting with a timer, taking it as your order to increase the sadhan time, but it is like I wait for the time to get over. It rarely happens that I do not experience any kriya-like crawling movements at the forehead or near the heart, some choking feeling in my throat, some lightning pain in the lower abdomen region, or heaviness in the head. Still, even those don't make me sit and experience the kriyas.

I know that I need to sit longer for my own progress, but again I say to myself that it will happen when it has to. I don't know if I am finding an excuse in the name of free will. Meanwhile, I focus on Guru Pratima (image) and chant the mantra whenever possible. I even felt like asking how people get to this level of sitting in sadhan for 3 to 4 hours. Then again, I thought it was unique for everyone. I even find it difficult to sit in the correct posture.

Kriyas can be experienced all the time. Even while writing this, something is crawling in the back region. Am I talking with the shakti or Guru Ji real, or is it just an illusion I have created to soothe my mind? I even took a break of 3 days, and when I felt ready, I started again. Now also, I hardly sat for 5 minutes and got up to ask you; but now I don't know what the question was? Am I just sharing what is happening to me, or am I looking for an answer to a question I don't know?

My response: Whatever you are experiencing is only kriyas, including your emotions in mind. You are not doing anything wrong. You don't have to do anything else either. All you need to do is not worry too much about the duration of your sadhan. I said that you just give it that extra push and try to stretch out the duration of your sadhan. It doesn't mean that you forcibly try and do sadhan. It is against the principles of Shaktipat sadhan or sadhan dharma to do sadhan by force. Let it happen naturally. As long as you continue with persistence regularly, there is nothing to worry about.

Intuitive messages during sadhan

Question: A practitioner: I had a most profound experience today. While meditating, I received a very dominant message about my father. I was suddenly brought to my knees. Overcome by grief and I started sobbing uncontrollably.

Secrets of Shaktipat and Kundalini Yoga

Then, this message cut through it all. In my ear, it told me he was a very powerful wanderer who had been overcome by negative entities and was in peril of not awakening in this incarnation. The message was to awaken him remotely. I tried, but I have no idea. I humbly ask for any assistance that will not infringe on the free will of my father.

My response: Where is your father now, and how old is he? Please understand that you can't give him Shaktipat initiation because it doesn't work that way. Therefore, there is no point in trying to do that. Secondly, whatever message you say you have received is the cleaning of your own karma from your subconscious mind. Perhaps your inner desire accumulated in your subconscious mind is now getting purged out during meditation.

Question: A practitioner: I could sit for the most extended duration of 3 Hr 40 minutes with your blessing. The whole session was full of physical kriyas, motions, etc. At the same time, like a perfect 2-in-1 mind, always focused on expressing myself, it kept bringing me to all the important people in my current life. People from profession or home and from relationship and growth perspectives! It went to the extent of giving a strategic directive on how it should be done. Towards the end, very heavy vibrations were on my head, so fast that I heard a whooshing sound and then blankness for some time. There were pockets of complete silence and blankness. Overall, the sadhan was terrific.

My question - all actions that come out of sadhan which make a lot of sense in practical life to adopt. Is that something we should embrace, or is it just a kriya and should be released from the mind post the sadhan. Your guidance on this would greatly help, as I keep getting these insights almost daily, but I don't know how to process these insights.

My response: Excellent; I am pleased to see your progress. All the internal contradictions and complexities about various aspects of life get resolved during sadhan. This is the direct result of cleaning your karma pertaining to multiple aspects. That is how a practitioner gets answers to all his questions internally. That is the essence of yoga practice. All the knowledge one seeks is within.

Therefore, all that is required is to remove the obstructions or impurities from the mind. That is precisely what happens during the sadhan. Of course, all the rising thoughts are kriyas only manifesting to clean up your past karmas. Just continue with your practice the same way. It is a lifelong journey. Slowly and steadily, the mind undergoes the transformation. However, please don't focus on adopting any insights you received during sadhan. As such, you would be taking appropriate actions based on your understanding during daily chores.

Question: Same practitioner: Could you shed light on actions or wisdom arising out of sadhan? Is it okay to act on it, or should we simply discard all the experience post sadhan as it was only for mental resolution and wisdom and nothing beyond that? Would acting upon it create karma, and would the cycle go on?

My response: Actually, the wisdom which arises out of sadhan will inspire you to remain a silent spectator to everything. In a nutshell, it inspires you not to do anything at all. You are inspired to stay dispassionate about whatever thoughts arise in your mind. SO, BE IT. That is the kind of attitude that gets developed in your mind.

Obviously, your actions while engaged in the external world will also be akin to the same. That means you don't get disturbed as such by anything. However, everyone needs to undertake actions obviously. They need not be about complex issues in life. They encompass the entire spectrum of activities. Because you need to perform certain karmas to maintain your body, like daily ablutions, eating, drinking, wearing clothes, sleeping, and working to earn your food. Even if it amounts to begging or gathering roots and fruits in a forest, like in the good old days. These karmas are inescapable. A practitioner sometimes gets impacted by such fresh karma if adequate dispassion is not exercised.

However, it doesn't matter if they accumulate in mind once again. It will be relatively easier to clean them later during sadhan. The same thing applies to the so-called difficult karmas in modern life. If you try and sharply discern, you will realize there is no difference between the good old and contemporary lifestyles. The essence remains the same. These external karmas will also happen as kriyas. You don't get any clarity during the sadhan regarding the correct way to take action.

There is nothing known as perfect action. Action is action or karma when tinged with egoism. Whether seemingly a noble action or sinful or unethical or humane or anything else is simply TRASH. Of course, when dispassion is developed as a result of sadhan, those karmas or actions cease to be karmas or actions since they no longer bind you. Therefore, that is the answer to your above question.

The knowledge will get revealed to you that everything is simply TRASH. It is not what you think is a PERFECT ACTION. I am unsure whether I have managed to convey the idea to you. If not, please feel free to ask me.

The crux of the matter is that a practitioner needs to develop dispassion for this world while remaining within the illusionary realm itself. It is akin to repairing a patch of a busy road in a city. You can't stop the traffic, yet manage to fix it somehow. That is a term of reference or condition imposed on you. The same is true when you try to free yourself from the accumulated karma. The awakened kundalini energy will do that skillful management of your life. Otherwise, it is simply not possible for a human being to do it based on egoistic control of his or her life. It is actually a simple issue if a practitioner can exercise self-surrender.

Misunderstanding sadhan as meditation

Question: A practitioner: I have started going deep in dhyan while doing sadhan. I reach an almost thoughtless stage. What should I do to go deeper and open more layers in dhyan? What point should I focus on to enter the next step for deep meditation? If I keep my awareness on my navel instead of on my mind and heart, I am able to surrender and focus more. My mind also vanishes without any struggle. I feel vast and deep when I keep my awareness of the navel.

My response: I think you are not doing sadhan. What you are trying to do is meditation. In our path, sadhan or practice means to do nothing. To remain in a state of witness as a mute spectator! You are mixing up the techniques in independent yoga systems like Ashtanga Yoga or Raja Yoga with Shaktipat. In our path, you are supposed to focus only on your Guru and chant the mantra. If your mind gets diverted as happening in your case, then just let it be so. Just keep observing it.

You can't go into deeper levels of samadhi without cleaning your karmas. It is only a temporary phenomenon if you have been experiencing it. You must have done such meditation practices in your previous or current life. Even those sensual impressions accumulated in your subconscious mind pertaining to meditation need to be cleaned up after Shaktipat. I hope you understand now. Kindly read my book on questions and answers compiled. All these ideas will become clear. Therefore, there is nothing to be done to get to deeper levels. It doesn't happen that way by any of your efforts. It occurs naturally as your karma is cleaned.

Correct way of doing sadhan

Question: A practitioner: When we do sadhan, we must focus on mantra and Guru. After starting sadhan, in no time, the mantra we are chanting is going on inside. On the other hand, instead of focussing on Guru so many flashes, internal discussions begin taking place.

Secrets of Shaktipat and Kundalini Yoga

My response: That is okay. That is the way to do sadhan. It is adequate if you invoke Guru for a few minutes and then focus on chanting of mantra. Even mantra may also come to a stop after kriyas begin. But whatever happens, must happen naturally. If thoughts arise in your mind during sadhan, then just keep observing them. Don't try to remember your Guru or mantra again, and stop those thoughts. That is the correct way of doing sadhan. Please remember that meditation on your Guru or mantra is only to kick start the manifestation of kriyas. In the end, even the bond with your Guru also must come to an end. That may happen at advanced stages of your spiritual growth.

Question: Same practitioner: How does sadhan kill karma?

My response: By way of kriyas in all forms like mental, physical, emotional, visual, sensual, etc. It all comes out one last time in front of you in sadhan for cleansing.

Question: A practitioner: Is it okay to meditate on balancing the Chakras?

My response: It is not required because, in our path, you are not supposed to focus your mind on anything while kriyas are happening. Before the kriyas kick start, you are required to focus on your Guru and the mantra. However, there is no harm if you focus your mind on the Chakras, but it is not required at all. It is like going back to high school from college. I hope you understand my message.

Question: A practitioner: Although I understand it is in a dualistic sense. Can you share the presiding deity whose blessings we should seek when we do Shaktipat meditation?

My response: Your Guru is the only deity here. Because religion no longer has any relevance on the path of yoga! Instead, it will slow down your progress. You know that people from all religions have taken Shaktipat deeksha from me. What will happen to them? Should I tell them to convert to Hinduism? And which deity should they pick up? Or do you say that they are not entitled to divine grace or salvation?

Therefore, please understand this from this perspective. Worshipping deities in religion is only a temporary phenomenon. Not an end. YOU are the end. Self-realization is the end. Even your relationship with your Guru is severed at the end. But for the time being, since you are under the spell of dualism, please worship the Guru or the Guru tattva. Since that Guru tattva has no form like motherhood, please worship your own Guru in physical form.

Question: Same practitioner: Also, when I sit for sadhan and try to focus on your picture, my mind drifts away, or something comes and disturbs my focus, or at times, I fall asleep while repeating the mantra; your insight, please.

My response: Just let it be so. Just remain a mute spectator and observe your thoughts in a state of witness. However, during the other times when you are not sitting in meditation, please cultivate the habit of remembering your Guru as many times as possible from the time you wake up and till you go off to sleep. Every time you remember the physical form of your Guru, you automatically invoke cosmic power. You will get significantly benefitted by this. Whatever you eat or drink or do, offer it to your Guru first. That is the thumb rule.

Question: A practitioner: I continuously meditate and do Pranayam daily. I always focus on each of the 7 Chakras. I felt a lot of energy revolving around me. There was a sudden shock-like feeling in my body towards my shoulders. Guru Ji told me that it may be a sudden sensation of kriya, but I felt these sudden shocks in my dream. As if somebody was pushing me from inside with an externally invisible force of action. I gained experience focusing on all seven Chakras within one full breath (Inhale and Exhale). When I finished my meditation, I observed that my soul connected with some Super Soul. I always felt my energy is meeting with Supreme energy through the Sahasrara Chakra. At this point, I do feel extreme happiness and harmony. My brain totally relaxed with this continuous action.

My response: Very nice; glad to see your progress. However, please remember that you don't have to focus on any Chakras or breathing intake during meditation. It is not meditation that you are supposed to do here. It is called sadhan, TO DO NOTHING.

Therefore, after offering your respects to the Gurus, focus on the mantra given to you and your Guru. If kriyas manifest and your mind gets diverted, then keep observing the kriyas like a silent spectator. Please don't try to do anything else. It is not required at all. Whatever has to happen in your body will now occur in an automatic mode and not by your efforts. You will only slow down the awakened kundalini energy if you try to focus your mind on unnecessary things like; Chakras etc. Just surrender yourself completely and keep observing the kriyas.

Question: A practitioner: I have been trying to focus on your image while doing sadhan, but I see a lot of other visions and pictures. Do I have to re-focus on your image or just go with the flow?

My response: Initially, focus your mind on your Guru's image. After that, if you see other visions, let it be so. Just keep observing those visions as a silent spectator. Those visions are kriyas only. You don't have to re-focus your mind on your Guru. Just go with the flow.

Question: A practitioner: For the last two days, I haven't been able to concentrate during sadhan. I am following all the instructions at the time of sadhan. After two hours, my mind is not calm, and sometimes my head moves toward the front. After sadhan, I feel dizzy. One day I went to sleep for some time after sadhan. Am I doing anything wrong?

My response: You are concentrating on what? You are not supposed to focus on anything other than the chanting of the mantra. That is also bound to halt after some time due to kriyas. The same thing applies to focusing your mind on your Guru initially. Your attention is bound to get diverted after some time. After that, you are supposed to remain in a state of witness as a mute spectator.

Just observe the kriyas, whether they are physical or mental. Many thoughts arise in your mind due to the churning effect of the awakened kundalini energy. Due to this, your mind will not be calm. The more thoughts that arise in your mind, the more cleaning occurs. You can't expect to reach a blissful state of thoughtlessness yet.

It is also quite normal to experience heaviness in the head both during and after meditation. This is caused by solid karma opposing the awakened kundalini energy. When cleaned, the effect is felt as one sort of heaviness in the cerebral region. It is also normal to go off to sleep after sadhan due to this cerebral activity. Therefore, I have not understood your doubt regarding this.

Please read the book of the compiled questions and answers. I have repeatedly explained these things earlier. If you read the book, most of your doubts will be answered. Otherwise, I will have to keep on repeating these things. Head going forward is also a normal kriya. Please rephrase your question again since I don't understand your message clearly.

Question: A practitioner: This is a fundamental doubt. How do we practice sadhan? I find it challenging to focus simultaneously on the mantra and Guru Ji!'s face. Can I practice focussing on the breath, as you have suggested? Can I also practice witnessing the thoughts and sensations in my body?

My response: You need to focus on your Guru and mantra only. If kriyas begin and the mantra stops on its own, then only focus on the kriyas and remain in a state of witness. Otherwise, you should not focus on your breathing or

Secrets of Shaktipat and Kundalini Yoga

anything else. That is not our path. Please understand that whatever has to happen will happen only through your Guru.

Focusing on your Guru is not a mere symbolic requirement. It is a mandatory requirement. Shakthipat has happened for you through your Guru. Therefore, cosmic power is invoked automatically when you focus on your Guru. Similarly, cosmic energy is invoked whenever you focus your mind on your mantra. Please don't mix up the literature about other independent yoga systems like Ashtanga or Raja yoga with Shakthipat. Those techniques are different.

Please read the compiled questions and answers. Just surrender yourself entirely to your Guru and follow the teachings of Shakthipat. I can't give you permission to do something as per your wish, please. Because what you are suggesting doesn't pertain to our path. If you cannot focus on your Guru and mantra, it shows that your mind cannot exercise self-surrender. The only remedy is a regular practice.

Question: A practitioner: Today was my 3rd day after I received Shaktipat deeksha. This time I felt some sensation slowly building and moving up toward Manipura chakra. It wasn't instantaneous, but like very, very slow that you don't understand whether it is moving. But after some time, I realized yes something was there. And as I opened my eyes, I could feel either cold or getting colder from root to Manipur chakra.

The meditation lasted for only 45 minutes. During my meditation, whenever I see very bright light filling up the entire place, I suddenly get scared and come out of that state. It has been happening for past so many times.

My response: That is called resisting the kriyas. I have repeatedly been saying the same thing constantly. Please don't try to resist the kriyas, whatever they may be. They obviously pertain to all nine categories of human emotions. Usually, people tend to enjoy the pleasant kriyas by emotionally getting attached to them. They instead try to seek to experience the same type of kriyas again and again.

As a result, they accumulate as new karma, although it is relatively easier to clear them later during the sadhan. Similarly, it can happen oppositely also when a practitioner tries to resist the unpleasant kriyas. In this case, the karmas don't get cleaned up. They might get cleaned up a little, but as soon as the practitioner starts resisting them due to fear, shyness, disgust, intellectual dilemma, physical pain, or anything else; obviously, kriyas will stop immediately. The only remedy for this is total self-surrender to your Guru.

This self-surrender, in turn, arises only when you start trusting your Guru. This trust in your Guru develops when you start having faith in the Guru. Therefore, finally, everything boils down to faith. If this faith is not there, then nothing is there. Haven't I given some explanation about it in my first book? It seems you forgot the essence of it. Therefore, please reread it if possible.

Falling asleep during sadhan

Question: A practitioner: I am falling asleep while doing sadhan. Is it good or bad for progress? Can we call it yoga Nidra?

My response: Falling asleep during sadhan is an obstacle for you. It is not good for progress, obviously. However, some amount of negative karma would have got washed away by that act of falling asleep. For this, you need to understand why obstacles are created for practitioners in the first place, including falling asleep. For this, kindly read my book on the compiled questions and answers. This subject has been discussed several times already. It is not yoga, Nidra, as you mentioned.

Frankly, I have no idea about that term myself. Therefore, kindly refrain from thinking about such kinds of things. Whatever the term yoga Nidra means is irrelevant. What matters is the burning down of your karma. This is possible only during sadhan and when you are fully awake. Because karmas are destroyed or created only during the waking state of mind! Therefore, please do anything to remain awake only during sadhan.

Take a small nap or have sound sleep before you sit for sadhan. Similarly, don't sit for sadhan after eating any main meal. Please give it a gap of at least 3 hours. Similarly, don't sit for sadhan when you are tired. These are some of the tips to avoid falling asleep during sadhan. Please be careful not to fall into illusionary ideas of your spiritual progress by thinking about exotic terminologies like yoga Nidra etc. which you find on the internet or in books.

Increasing duration of sadhan

Question: A practitioner: I am able to do sadhan from 30 minutes to a maximum of 55 minutes. During this time, kriyas, pranayam, and various mudras manifest regularly. The kriyas are more subtle and not so acrobatic, if I may say. My question is, why do eyes open at different intervals in a flash of a moment. Sometimes after this moment, body sensations are felt. I usually stop with my "naman" to Gurus expressing my gratitude for guiding me to this path. Is it that the cosmic energy guides the duration of sadhan, or do I need to continue after this flash eye-opening, which happens without any stimulus? All the while, I experience that the body is in auto-pilot mode, and I am the witness. Please guide me on overcoming the time factor to increase the duration of sadhan.

My response: Yes, the duration of sadhan is also controlled by the cosmic energy of regular practitioners in their sadhan. Therefore, please don't worry about it too much. Just let the sadhan happen naturally. However, I keep recommending slowly increasing the practice duration but don't forcefully do it either.

Question: A practitioner: I am very interested in how some people struggle to sit for long periods of sadhan and then others can sit for a long time, 3-4 hrs. What happens internally here? Is the cosmic energy in a different state, or is the mind more of a Satvic state that allows the cosmic energy to do its work?

My response: Actually, it is under the control of the awakened kundalini energy. The fructification of "asan," or the posture, gets affected naturally as one progresses. However, a practitioner shouldn't be lethargic under the excuse of this principle. It is your internal state. Practitioners can change the position of their legs or stretch them once in a while if required. However, during intense and deep sadhan, this requirement may not be necessary. Lastly, please remember that TIME appears to vanish, just like that, for a practitioner in deep meditation. That means TIME, as we all know it to be an absolute, ceases to be so for a practitioner in deep sadhan. That is how we keep hearing stories about great sages who can remain seated in deep meditation for long hours, days, months, or years.

Question: A practitioner: How to increase the sadhan time? I cannot sit for more than an hour. How do I improve it?

My response: Please don't worry about it too much. Actually, it is under the control of the awakened kundalini energy itself. However, from your side, try and stretch the duration a little bit without trying to force it. Please do follow some tips. Try and sit for sadhan after resting or waking up from sleep. Please don't try to sit for sadhan when you are tired or after returning back from work.

Next, please try and sit for sadhan on an empty stomach or after a gap of at least three hours if you have eaten any main meal. However, you can always sit for sadhan after light refreshments, etc. Also, please try and empty your bowels before sitting for sadhan. Next, please sit for sadhan after

Secrets of Shaktipat and Kundalini Yoga

taking a bath if possible. Otherwise, there is no restriction as such concerning bathing. It might help you a little.

Next, try and sit for sadhan at a fixed time and place. As a result, the sheer force of the habit will carry you forward whenever you don't feel like doing sadhan. Next, always try and focus your mind on your Guru. This will help you in getting inspired to do sadhan. There are some excellent books on Shaktipat written by some of our Gurus. Most of these books are available in Hindi. Otherwise, a few books are available in English, Telugu, and Marathi. You must read such books. They will inspire you to do sadhan. They have a powerful impact on the practitioners. Some of our practitioners have managed to buy a set of those books. Otherwise, please read my book as many times as possible. Some of our members have read it around 10-15 times. Therefore, you must follow some of the above tips, at least if not all.

Lastly, please remember that you can always try and do some service to your Guru, which helps keep you inspired on the path of yoga. This service could be anything as per your aptitude. Even offering a cup of coffee, tea, water, food, fruits, or sweets to your Guru every time before you eat is considered a service.

Similarly, you can post something on the lineage of the Shaktipat Order, or spreading the message is also considered such a service. If you are a painter, you can try and paint the Gurus, or if you happen to be a writer, you can write something.

Otherwise, simply remembering the Guru is also very helpful. Please do it at your convenience and aptitude. That is how you end up attracting divine grace. Please understand the simple logic that the Guru, the mantra, or the cosmic energy is of the same form. Therefore, do whatever you can and attract grace. Otherwise, divine blessings are always radiating on you equally all the time.

Colonel T Sreenivasulu

Question: A practitioner: For many days I have observed that many sadhaks like to prolong their sadhan time, as advised by you. Many sadhaks are doing it even for 4 hours and more, giving the impression that there is some competition among them. Please elaborate more on the quality of sadhan rather than the long hours of sadhan. Does sitting longer hours more beneficial for sadhak, or sadhan with complete dedication and surrender will benefit more.

It seems people are putting more physical strength into the sadhan rather than being into one. Please clarify this, as many others must be confused about what to do and what not to do? Moreover, what should be the ultimate goal of the sadhak?

My response: First, sitting for sadhan in meditative posture is more of a formality that needs to be undergone compulsorily and regularly. Otherwise, after Shaktipat initiation, a person doesn't do anything. Cleaning of karmas goes on round the clock. Some of our practitioners have reported that kriyas, like vibrations, etc., are taking place even while not doing any sadhan.

In an ideal situation, every moment of life becomes sadhan provided the practitioner exercises self-surrender and dispassion while undergoing the daily chores. However, formally sitting for sadhan helps a practitioner in several ways. First of all, you cultivate the force of habit. Secondly, you are not trapped in lethargy under the excuse that it is the divine power that is controlling your destiny. Although it is true, please also understand that a practitioner is still under the spell of the Maya or illusion. That means on one side, the same cosmic power is dragging you back into the Maya and also simultaneously cleaning your karmas.

In the advanced stages of yoga practice, a practitioner is always deemed to be in sadhan. However, he doesn't formally sit for sadhan. Therefore, please understand this issue from this perspective.

Secrets of Shaktipat and Kundalini Yoga

Obviously, the quality of sadhan means exercising self-surrender and being in a state of witness. If you can do it efficiently, you are as such in sadhan only all the time. In contrast, if you can't do it, it is better to remain seated formally and do sadhan as much as possible. Haven't you heard of people sitting in meditation continuously for long hours or days or months, or even years?

As a practitioner advances in yoga, even the requirement of food and water is taken care of. There is something known as "Amrit Dhara" or the stream of ambrosia which is supposed to start getting excreted from the upper side of the larynx and which keeps the body alive by nourishing it. Therefore, there is no end to sadhan. Both quality and duration are equally important.

In order to cater to all kinds of practitioners with different abilities to sit for sadhan, it is suggested that you practice as much as possible and as many times as possible. Exercise self-surrender as much as you can.

Further, please remember that the awakened kundalini energy starts controlling the sadhan for a practitioner. However, one shouldn't take shelter under this excuse and be lethargic. It is better to go in for the overkill rather than falling short. That is why I encourage practitioners to give it a slight extra nudge and stretch the sadhan duration. At the same time, sadhan is not supposed to be done forcefully, either. Just try and maintain this delicate balance. Neither be lethargic nor force it.

Lastly, please don't compare your sadhan with that of others. Who knows, you may be already in a much more advanced state than the others!

However, I intend to inspire all those practitioners who might be lethargic in doing sadhan that I try to show them the example of others who practice for long hours.

Sometimes I, too, get inspired to do sadhan when I see some of you doing it for a long time. This is the advantage of being in an Ashram. So, that everyone gets inspired by others. There is no competition here. It is all about flowing with the group so that the others take even an average practitioner. I hope I have been able to convey the idea to you.

Question: Comment from another practitioner on the above question: It is a very pertinent question even I was curious as to why and how that would affect and why that aspiration? An answer to that was in one of the responses from Guru Ji, where he indicated that the quality of kriyas and experience change significantly or start to change. In my view, this indicates that high-level karmas are getting cleared and kriyas are getting subtler.

Hence, I was inspired to start fine-tuning my own sadhan, and in the last 3 days, I have been able to go to 4 hours mark. But I have been consciously trying to increase the time for a long time but never could do it. By forcing myself, and technically can't just sit without kriyas for so long and do nothing. My bit on this, but I would love to hear from Gurudev on this, as this is a common aspiration most of us have to keep increasing the time and get into samadhi ultimately.

My response: I hope your query is also addressed by the above reply. Just focus your mind internally. It is easier to do it while sitting in sadhan rather than taking shelter under the pretext that you are in sadhan only while you are busy with the daily chores. Therefore, please do sadhan as much as possible and as often as possible. Also, ensure quality by exercising self-surrender as much as you can.

There is nothing known as a perfect sadhan either. Perhaps only God can do it if he happens to be in human form. Although as per yoga texts, God can't exist in such human form and also do perfect sadhan. I have no idea about those divine incarnations who did it. Therefore, just focus on sadhan without trying to understand the mechanics of it intellectually. I would like to inform all sadhaks that please don't shy away from stopping the sadhan temporarily for a day or two or even several days if kriyas occur aggressively and you are not comfortable.

I have been making some practitioners stop doing their sadhan on several occasions. However, I don't make a public announcement of it often because I fear it might send a wrong signal to others. It might inspire some lethargic practitioners to make excuses for not doing sadhan.

Question: A practitioner: I need your guidance and blessings, please. Since the lockdown, I have consciously worked on increasing the sadhan time from 5-6 hours each day in 4 sessions. For the last 1 week, I have been able to get to 7 hours each day with 3 sessions. Session 1 of 5 hours - from 4:30 am to 9:30 am; sessions 2 and 3 are 1-1.5 hours each in the afternoon and evening. I need your support and guidance to fine-tune the first session of 5 hours, and I have observed the following: -

1) 5 hours session - kriyas were happening throughout the session but have become much softer or smoother, with no sudden jerks, etc. Is it okay, or should I break the session into 2 of 2.5 hours each?

2) I get into yoga Nidra almost on all 5 occasions varying between 40 minutes to 1.5 hours. Is it okay, or how to reduce this?

3) I could start earlier as I initially started my sadhan at 3:40 am but delayed it. I now take a bath and then start my session at 4:30 am.

4) My Mind is calmer, but I still do not get calm enough to lose track of time or go into shoonya. Any guidance on this would greatly help.

5) Please let me know if I am overdoing or rushing things, as I am trying to take advantage of the lockdown situation. I am

also not impacting my family life adversely, as my sessions end before my family's day starts.

My response: Obviously, kriyas will not always manifest in the same way. Sometimes they are aggressive, and sometimes they are very mild. But the most important thing is not to do sadhan forcefully. It all depends upon you. You are the best judge. If you feel like stopping it, please do so. Don't try to stretch it forcefully.

I have been telling some of the practitioners to increase the duration of their practice. I have observed that it is not adequate for them. The advice to stretch out the duration of practice is meant for lethargic type practitioners, including myself. Still, you don't have to follow it. Next, please don't try to stop the sadhan forcefully. You need to strike that delicate balance yourself.

Regarding splitting the sadhan into several sessions, there is no fixed rule. You can do it at your convenience. In a nutshell, please feel free. Don't be lethargic, and don't forcefully do it. I hope you got the idea now.

Question: A practitioner: I have increased my sadhan duration in this lockdown period from 40 minutes to 90 minutes. I have energy flow in my arms and third eye. I had a vision of white and other colors. My main difficulty during sadhan is the numbness I get in my right leg. Due to that, 3-4 times, I am stretching my leg. Is this numbness also kriya? How to overcome this problem so that I can increase my sadhan duration? Please advise me.

My response: Numbness in the leg is due to usual reasons. Usually happens during meditation. Just try and adjust your legs. Happens typically due to some nerve getting pressed etc. Please don't worry about it too much. In any case, you can always stretch your legs and change their position. But please don't try to sit in the same position forcefully.

Taking breaks during sadhan

Secrets of Shaktipat and Kundalini Yoga

Question: A practitioner: Yesterday, I started my sadhan at 9:00 PM and finished by 1:05 AM local time here. It was past 4 hrs of sadhan. So, I couldn't inform you about joining in at the time of group meditation; by that time, I was already in deep sadhan. I experienced kriyas of the drooping head and neck, itching on my face, occasional pains, and a current flowing in the heart, stomach, neck, left ribs, navel, left wrist, and jerks on my right hand. I felt pressure alternatively on the left and right ear. Sometimes the pressure was heavy. My throat Chakra was very active throughout the sadhan. Feelings of heaviness, dryness, thirst, and even choking in the throat area were there. At times I felt like playing the musical instrument "Veena." I felt a surge of energy from my throat to the Crown Chakra with heavy vibrations on the Crown Chakra. Felt very heavy-headed. After 4 hrs of sadhan, I felt hungry. I took a sip of water and went to sleep. Can we drink water with closed eyes during sadhan due to extreme thirst? Usually, I take water before and after sadhan. Please Guide.

My response: Very nice. Yes, you can drink water if you feel thirsty in between. In our path, it is not meditation that is done. It is called sadhan. Therefore, there is no restriction on taking a break in between. You don't even have to keep your eyes closed while drinking water. You can open your eyes, take a break if you wish, and resume your practice once again. I am pleased to see your progress. Please continue with your practice the same way.

Sadhan related issues

Question: A practitioner: This morning in my practice, I was visited by several images and people that looked like spirits. Faces and bodies I did not recognize, even children coming to me, some were disfigured, and some were normal. What are these? Are these due to karma? They seem to exist in another world that I was looking into?

My response: Such kinds of visions during sadhan are normal. Obviously, accumulated karmic impressions are getting cleaned. Please understand that such visions are the output of all the accumulated karmic junk. It doesn't necessarily mean that you had direct experience with such visions. It could have been the mixed-up karmic stuff getting cleaned out. Just keep observing them like a silent spectator. Otherwise, they don't foretell anything about future events either.

Question: A practitioner: Today's sadhan lasted for 4.5 hours. Since the start, I got prompted to be in a lying position. I experienced many kriyas like; force around the heart and Vishuddhi Chakras. A lot of visions, especially giving a vertigo-like feeling. Most of the visions had more than 3 dimensions; it looked like I had astral projection. My question: Is it normal to get into a lying position for the whole duration and not have physical kriyas.

My response: Yes, it is okay if you are practicing in a lying position. Physical kriyas may or may not happen. There are five different sheaths covering the soul. Obviously, everyone has karma accumulated which pertains to all five sheaths. As a result, kriyas will manifest in all five sheaths to clean up the respective karmas. Sometimes, the karmas being cleaned are not very strongly accumulated. In that case, a practitioner may not experience any physical or mental kriyas, or they could be very mild, and you may not notice.

In this connection, please remember that Shaktipat is like an express train. You will not see the minor stations en route while you are speeding past them on the express train. In contrast, if you are moving in a slow train, you will see all those intermediate stations. The same is the case here also. Therefore, please don't bother about the kriyas at all.

Question: A practitioner: The physical kriyas were very little for me. Right from the beginning, they were always emotional. For example, you told me I was doing something which nobody else did or failed at a very simple thing.

Secrets of Shaktipat and Kundalini Yoga

Cleaning emotional karmas of praise and abuse I have experienced both bizarrely and clearly.

My response: Very nice. Yes, that is how the cleaning of karma is affected. It all depends upon the kind of karma accumulated by the practitioners. Sometimes practitioners are not satisfied since they don't experience gross physical kriyas. That is against the principle of sadhan after Shaktipat initiation. A practitioner should not seek a particular set of kriyas or resist others. The focus should be internal, like a mute spectator. When practitioners can exercise such a kind of inner focus, they will understand the finer kriyas taking place.

Gross physical kriyas will stop at some stage or the other, in any case. The finer cleaning of emotions takes a very long time. It is akin to cleaning a dirty blanket. Initially, it is easier to dust it out of the gross impurities. Later, it takes a prolonged period to free the finer impurities from the blanket. From this perspective, cleaning the mind takes a very long time. Primarily the ego-related kriyas and those of the intellect are too fine. It is difficult to distinguish between kriya and karma. However, for a regular practitioner, that difference will get revealed internally, but only for regular practitioners. Otherwise, there is a risk of misunderstanding the new karmas as kriyas. I am pleased to see you practicing regularly. Please continue with your practice the same way. As a cardiologist, you must be busy nowadays, mainly due to the coronavirus. Please take care since you are exposed more.

Question: A practitioner: Why is there always a lot of water in the mouth during sadhan?

My response: It is a type of kriya only. It happens not only during sadhan but also continuously round the clock when it starts. Usually, the process goes on for one or two days sometimes and then stops. Again, it may begin intermittently after several days or weeks. The flavor of the water generating inside the mouth is also slightly different from the usual phlegm. A little bit of sweetness can be felt.

Question: A practitioner: Today's session lasted 30-35 minutes. Started and ended with prayers to Guru Jis. I couldn't concentrate totally. Thoughts about my lover kept bothering me. Need your help. The first three days were going great. Yesterday and today, both these days are not up to the mark. I could not even achieve basic concentration. How to overcome this? What am I doing wrong?

My response: I have now answered a query about thoughts arising during the sadhan. Please read it. Also, please read the compiled questions and answers book I shared earlier. That book will answer a lot of your questions. In our path, we are not doing meditation. It is called sadhan. Whatever kriya happens in your body or mind is no longer under your control. However, the kriyas will become fresh karmas if you get too passionate about them. The same is the case with you also. Just remember this much.

Otherwise, thoughts arising in your mind are kriyas only. The more they arise, the more of your karma gets cleaned up. Please don't worry that you are not able to enjoy blissful meditation yet. That means you are deliberately trying to seek pleasurable kriyas. You must bother about freeing yourself from accumulated karma or sensual impressions. Whether they are pleasant or unpleasant should not matter. Just allow them to arise in your mind. Slowly they start dying down. That is the essence of sadhan. I hope you understand now.

Question: A practitioner: When the mind is uneasy or unrestrained, then sitting in sadhan to calm it will amount to new karma? What should one do to settle a tense mind?

My response: Forcefully doing sadhan amounts to fresh karma only since it will be ego based. Next, calming the mind will only happen naturally as your karma is cleaned. Otherwise, please focus on your Guru and exercise total self-surrender. That is the best way to calm your mind, although only temporarily.

Question: A practitioner: My sadhan lasted for only 40 minutes today. Started and ended with prayers to Gurus. Today after the prayer, the sensation started immediately at the third eye region. For some time, there were shadows of many people running in front of me. I couldn't recognize any of them; who were they? Then I was deep inside and couldn't feel my body/breathing. I was very light and in a happy mood. This feeling lasted for the majority of the time.

Lastly, I could see my lover laughing and in a happy mood as she could leave the house. She went to two of our common friends' houses. At the first house, she was offered something to drink. She clicked her pictures. Then she went to the second friend's house to pick up some bakery products. She was happy there too. I found her chatting with my friend and his family but could not see others in my vision. Till this point, I was in a happy mood also. And I could visualize the entire thing. Lastly, I could hear the pooja bells in a nearby house. And my eyes became wet. I was returning back to my body. Prayed to the Gurus and completed my sadhan. Before completing sadhan, I just said to Gurus that I am now surrendering myself to you and my eyes became wet.

My Questions:

Currently, my lover is only in our common friend's house. I have known about her schedule since yesterday night. She went at 10.50 am, and I started sadhan at 11.30 am. I am very possessive about her. Do the images of my lover that I see in the session, do they destroy my karma or build new karma? I could not see my other two friends or their family members in the house. I could only see my lover's happy and laughing face. How do I interpret this?

Her schedule was not decided as to whose place she was going to first. I imagined her to be visiting one particular friend's place first and then to the next place. In the first place, I could see the bakery van also, but I could not see anything else. Are these my thoughts? Am I creating new karma?

Is it my intuition? Am I doing visualization? Though I am very possessive about my lover, I feel very calm now. Otherwise, I am very much anxious waiting for her.

As of now, I have no worries or anxiety about her. Images of my lover keep popping up in every session of my sadhan. Am I overthinking about her? Please help me to resolve this. My sadhan lasts for 40 / 50 minutes or so. Before deeksha, it used to be for more time. Sometimes it lasted for two hours also. But it was all about sitting calm and observing the breath and thoughts. What is the reason, and how can I improve my duration of sadhan? Sorry Guru Ji, to keep you bothering with my questions, but I don't have anyone except you to talk to.

My response: Whatever you are experiencing during your sadhan is basically kriyas. Sensual impressions accumulated in your subconscious mind are getting cleaned up. That is the bottom line. Please understand that after Shaktipat deeksha, your subconscious mind is subjected to a churning effect. As a result, all your thoughts, emotions, feelings, etc., start rushing out. That is why your visions and thoughts are flashed in your mind.

You might experience them even during a dream state also. This is the beginning of cleaning your karma. This will go on for a few days or weeks. But everything is happening for your good. To calm your mind. Soon you will start getting a totally different insight. Your mind is bound to undergo transformation. It will happen more rapidly if you practice more and exercise self-surrender. It will bring you peace and happiness.

Externally things may or may not change as you desire currently. But peace and happiness are assured for you,

Secrets of Shaktipat and Kundalini Yoga

provided you practice regularly. What else do you want? Rest everything else described by you are irrelevant.

However, knowing about your lover's movements is also obviously part of the kriyas only. Since your subconscious mind needs to get churned out, your lover and her friends are acting as a medium for you. Please don't worry about it at all. Everything is happening perfectly normally for you. Please don't bother about the duration of your sadhan at this stage. It has been only a few days since you have taken Shaktipat deeksha. Slowly it will increase on its own.

Question: A practitioner: This time, I have a rather stupid question. It has been on my mind for a couple of days. I observed that I was in a dual stage a few times during sadhan. I could clearly observe that kriyas were happening automatically without my effort. Still, at the same time, my mind was also in chatter mode. The mind is also churning thoughts. Most of the time, I bring it back to order by repeating the Guru mantra.

Sometimes, I miss invoking the Guru mantra, and this chatter goes on for a longer duration. The challenge is at that time, this chatter is useless. It is like thinking about job-related issues, solutions for Corona Virus, and World affairs like; the next move from China or USA in the current standoff. The question is should I nip the thoughts in the bud. Should I not pay attention and not allow it to grow further. Moreover, I feel doing this would be a voluntary interruption and forming new karmas. Or is it acceptable to do so? Please guide.

My response: You are not in any dual stage. All are kriyas only. Just forget to focus on your Guru and the mantra chanting during such moments. Just keep observing the mental and physical kriyas as a silent spectator. That is the correct way of doing sadhan. Let it be so even if you feel that you are deliberately trying to think about worldly issues. Those fresh karmas will be easier to clear later on. But please don't stop the thoughts since you may be unable to differentiate between kriya and karma.

Question: A practitioner: I have been doing sadhan off and on. Before last week, I felt very sleepy, tired, and somewhat depressed. Maybe because of the lockdown, or it was kriyas, as I have read similar experiences of sleepiness of the other practitioners. I don't know, so I took a break from my sadhan. I am fine now.

One thing I wanted to understand. When I begin my sadhan, within minutes, my mind is full of thoughts of people and situations from the past, present, and future. I am not sure if these thoughts are kriyas or distractions. I have read that you say these are kriyas, but even when I am not sitting down for sadhan, I experience these thoughts, so I don't understand. I usually try to bring my focus back to my mantra and your image. I am not experiencing the physical kriyas lately.

My response: After Shaktipat initiation sitting for sadhan is more of a formality, although it is to be followed compulsorily. As a result, many practitioners keep experiencing the kriyas around the clock. While a practitioner is engaged in worldly activities, it is challenging to remain in a state of witness as a mute spectator.

Therefore, neutralizing karmas is not done that efficiently, although kriyas go on while you are engaged in your daily routine. Further, new karma may accumulate since a practitioner is likely to be impacted emotionally during daily chores. Hence, it is suggested that practitioners formally sit for sadhan every day or regularly. While seated in sadhan, the mind is more in a state of witness, as you would be closing doors on the external world.

Regarding your doubt as to whether thoughts are kriyas, yes, they are kriyas only. The more thoughts arise, the better for you, but they should occur naturally. Then only your accumulated karmas in the subconscious mind are neutralized. You shouldn't deliberately try to think. There is a fragile line of difference between kriya and karma. When it comes to mental activity, it becomes difficult to distinguish between kriya and karma, but no need to worry about it. Even if new karma is accumulated, it will be relatively easy to get them cleared. All this is, however, applicable only when you are regular in your practice.

Otherwise, there is a tendency to view everything as a kriya while engaged in daily routine. Please don't worry about all this; just sit for sadhan regularly. Focus your mind on your Guru as frequently as possible every day. Even if you are not able to sit for sadhan, the recalling of Guru's image will offset to some extent. Physical kriyas may or may not always happen. You should be interested in cleaning up your karmas and not kriyas. Kriyas are only a means. They depend upon your accumulated karma.

Question: A practitioner: Is restlessness or an endless desire for experiencing kriya after Shaktipat, is also a kriya manifesting through in thought form? My mind has become restless as I am unaware of experiencing a kriya. But a part of me knows. It is just a bundle of thoughts rising in my mind. I am trying to look at it as a spectator. Not taking these thoughts seriously.

My response: As per the yoga texts, there are around 1,25,000 kinds of kriyas. Even thought pattern comes under that. Kriyas may happen the way you described. In the initial stages, kriyas may not manifest, but in later stages, you may experience them frequently. First, you must remember that we do not have only one layer of the physical body. Besides the gross physical body, we have two other significant layers of our body. Sukshma or subtle and Karan or causal bodies are the other two.

The kundalini energy is conscious and all-knowing. It works in many ways. Sometimes in the physical body and sometimes in other bodies wherein we cannot experience its impact as it works very subtly. Just do your sadhan with total dedication and not think of anything else. Kriyas will manifest to you as your karmas are neutralized.

Question: A practitioner: I have been doing Sadhan for almost two months. Since last week I have been chanting the Gayatri mantra, clapping, and neck rotations are also happening. Suppose I do sadhan early in the morning, after sadhan. In that case, I get into Shavasana and fall into a deep sleep for around 30 minutes to one hour.

My response: That is nice. If the Gayatri mantra is happening like a kriya, then let it happen. Other things are also kriyas. Continue your sadhan the same way. Sleeping after sadhan is a common thing that many sadhaks experience.

Question: A practitioner: I am back to regular Sadhan after two weeks of disruption. I am experiencing absolutely nothing. Even the vibrations and jerks I used to have been no longer happening.

My response: You may experience kriyas again after a few days. It is quite normal not to experience kriyas always during sadhan. Sometimes kriyas work in a very subtle way and our physical body may not sense it. Just do your sadhan without any expectation of kriyas. We cannot expect kriyas to manifest our way. They will manifest on their own based on your accumulated karma. Do sadhan regularly.

Question: A practitioner: Swami Shivom Tirth Ji says when kriyas aren't manifesting, one must follow severe spiritual discipline. I am having a very mild manifestation of kundalini. Should I follow any physical or spiritual discipline Guru Ji?

My response: Not required as such for you. But you need to focus your mind on your Guru always, please. It is not any symbolic requirement but rather a precise mathematical type requirement. Please understand this. It is not to the physical body of your Guru that you are offering your respects but to the Guru tattva or the essence of Guru. The secret of success in yoga practice is this only. The moment you comprehend the significance of this teaching, your spiritual growth begins rapidly. There is no other technique needed.

His Holiness must be referring to those cases where sadhaks lack this kind of devotion to their Guru. Suppose they happen to undergo some severe spiritual disciplines. In that case, their minds will obviously be subdued to self-surrender. That is the essence of it. But you don't have to undertake any such extreme measures. Make it a habit to remember your Guru from morning to night several times a day, before eating or doing something, etc. That is sufficient.

Question: A practitioner: What do I do if I can't perform sadhan one day for unavoidable reasons like traveling? How to compensate for it?

My response: Please don't worry about it. Just do it whenever it is possible for you.

Question: A practitioner: I have joined a new organization, as I informed you earlier. My previous employer has not paid my dues to date and avoiding me. But I am getting a lot of negative thoughts in the ordinary course. I am trying my best to divert my mind to remain non-emotional. Please advise being a sadhak in the normal course, can we restrict negative or positive thought processes.

My response: You don't have to do anything at all deliberately. Just go through the emotions, whether positive or negative, or anything else. Please don't restrict your thoughts. They are all kriyas only in the form of thoughts. Your subconscious mind is getting cleaned up from the accumulated karma. In this process, some of the emotions might accumulate once again as freak karmas since you may not be able to fully surrender.

But there is nothing to worry about it. Freshly accumulated karmas after Shakthipat deeksha are not that strong usually.

Therefore, it will be easier to clear them later during sadhan. But you must not resist such emotions.

Please understand that whatever you are experiencing is your accumulated karma only. You are only experiencing the reflection of your own subconscious mind. But soon, those karmas will get exhausted also. Nothing lasts permanently. But all this is applicable provided you are doing your sadhan regularly. Every day your karma will keep getting exhausted. So please don't worry and cheer up.

Question: A practitioner: The divine energy entered my spine and reached my throat and forehead. Is my kriya happening very fast? How much time should I do sadhan? I feel intoxicated most of the time.

My response: Sadhan is happening for you naturally as such. There is no need to do any extra sadhan as such. If you wish, you can sit for sadhan for some time. But please be careful. If kriyas are violent, then stop the sadhan immediately.

Question: A practitioner: Yeah, I was focusing on you and doing the mantra at times during the day but stopped a week ago. When doing this while not in sadhan, does that still activate Kundalini and work to purify the nadis like in sadhan? Also, now that you mentioned the kriyas dying down with karma, that happened with me because they are subtle, and it is mainly a trance-like state I get locked into. I also feel this and have had another person comment on this intensity from my eyes like a brightness. Sorry for all the questions.

My response: There is no need to worry about it. But you need to get back to sadhan at the earliest. Although kundalini energy will continue to work in your body, it will not be optimum since you are not doing sadhan regularly and your mind is engaged elsewhere. However, focusing on Guru's image and mantra during the normal time will help. But only to some extent.

Secrets of Shaktipat and Kundalini Yoga

Kriyas dying down is true with the cleaning of karmas. But it is too early for you to take shelter under this excuse for not doing sadhan regularly. The mind has a way of tricking the sadhaks into refraining from doing Sadhan. It creates all kinds of reasons internally, which appear very logical. But it is just illusionary excuses. A sadhak should be very careful about this.

Question: A practitioner: Today I felt something crawling sensation left the joint of my shoulder and hand to the back of my neck. This flowed in an upward direction, starting from the joint of my right hand. Another kriya happens when I sit still and observe. When I breathe out, I feel pressure on my Ajna chakra. I meditated for only 10 minutes Guru Ji, and I couldn't continue as I was meditating in the darkroom.

My head was rotating to the left, then left to right, and then clockwise. I felt my energy is so heavy in the outer part of my body, and it is going up with heaviness. I also felt heaviness above my neck to the top of my head. I also saw Trishul. But I got scared and stopped meditating then. Why was I got afraid, Guru ji?

My response: Excellent! These are all physical and mental kriyas. You don't need to be scared of anything. When it comes to the crown or head, you feel the heaviness. Seeing a Trishul is an auspicious sign. No need to be afraid. Please continue with your Sadhan.

Question: A practitioner: I want to inform you of one thing. I have mostly the same situation as yours before your Shaktipat initiation. I am financially bankrupt right now. But I am trying to come out of this situation. A few positive signs have come since I got Guru's grace.

For this reason, I am just wandering here and there. I am looking for some financial solutions. Sometimes I am very busy with these activities. And I couldn't do sadhan.

Colonel T Sreenivasulu

Today morning and also one more morning, sadhan couldn't be executed. I have two problems simultaneously, one financial and the other health issue. The health issue was not serious before I was into Shaktipat. But I was not feeling well once the kriya started. I don't understand why I continuously sweat heavily while in AC.

The kriya also never happened to me before the Shaktipat. I consider sweating as a part of kriya. But I am not very sure about it. You can guide me on this. But you know, Guru ji, I am associated with you because of going deeper and deeper into the spiritual journey. I mostly don't have any material desires by opting for this path.

I definitely will not deny that I don't have any material desire. Still, it is on an elementary level only. I worked so hard but still faced the issues. Actually, if I will also estimate myself as a third person, I should never face such problems. I have devoted a lot of time to my profession. And I never mislead anyone. There could be some minor mistakes I made. But those were only mistakes because I am a human being.

But in my profession, I helped many companies so that they could earn a lot of money. I am considered a very hard-working, brilliant, and honest person in my profession. But even then, if I am facing some issues, I am making some mistakes. So, I came to you on the journey of searching for my errors. When reading your book, one thing clicked with me; there is a call from God. The situation is because of that I am just not following the divine path. So, I realized that it is the path I should immediately opt for it. So, I surrendered to you.

I want to know if sweating a lot also could be a part of kriya. And I will be doing justice for the divine work given to me. Please, wait until I finish it. And I will not take much time. I have been busy for the last two days with many issues with bringing my business on track. And you know, as I promised you, I will launch my first product in October. I need to fulfill that promise which I made to my Guru.

My response: Sweating occurs as part of the kriyas usually. However, suppose you have been sweating during other times when not doing sadhan. In that case, you should also check out for any other health issues. Kriyas don't harm a person. That is the bottom line.

Regarding your personal problems in daily life, regular sadhan is the single solution for you. As you keep doing sadhan, your karmas also keep getting cleaned. As karma gets cleaned, your life will also get impacted. The net result will be the peace of mind. But you shouldn't expect life to unfold as per your desire; only the divine knows what can bring you peace of mind.

Therefore, divine power will grant you whatever is good for you. This is the crucial thing to understand. Hence, you need to exercise total self-surrender to the divinity or Guru. It is a test of your perseverance and self-surrender.

Question: A practitioner: I see my tarot cards while doing the sadhan. A vision and flashes of the tarot are there.

My response: There is no wonder in that. Because you must have accumulated karmas of Tarot reading. Since you are a Tarot reader, it is a well-known fact that many of those karmas must have accumulated in your subconscious mind. They are now being cleaned, obviously. I am pleased to see you doing sadhan regularly and kriyas being manifested for you.

Question: A practitioner: I just feel very lost. I am not doing sadhan also. I have no idea why I am doing this to myself. I am feeling very lost. I have been feeling a lot of guilt and irritation past two days. Please help me. I need help. I am getting diverted from my sadhan a lot. I don't feel like doing it, and I have no reason for feeling like this.

My response: Just focus on your Guru. There is nothing to worry about it as such. Just like the weather outside your home is not always constant, so is your mental condition. That is the medicine, the only medicine for mankind; you are not any exception. You have already been put on the right path. Therefore, there is no need to worry now. Please understand that it takes 7 days to get relief from the common cold. Please don't worry.

Medicine always tastes bitter. But that which tastes bitter initially will be sweet later, and it is the other way around always. Please understand that there is something known as a blockchain effect. Please focus on doing Guru Seva at least, in a materialistic sense, and for God's sake, don't let your mind entertain any doubts regarding the intentions of your Guru. When you focus your mind on your Guru and serve, then automatically, the first Guru of mankind, Lord Shiva, in the incarnation of Dakshinamurthi or the Guru tattva, is impacted.

It happens instantly, traveling through space and time. It is like time traveling instantly. Therefore, you need to understand the essence of this Guru Tattva. That is the only way to succeed in yoga. Success in yoga is the only way to peace of mind and happiness. Therefore, just focus your mind on your Guru. It may appear materialistic in nature trying to serve your physical Guru. But it is the technique involved here. Please don't focus on the kriyas and your own ego-based sadhan. This is where you are going wrong fundamentally. You don't do anything on the spiritual path. Rather you are supposed not to do anything. For that, you need to use a technique known as self-surrender.

Question: A practitioner: I have not been practicing for 2 weeks due to my dad's death. Yesterday I sat for 83 min in Sadhan; it felt like the lower part of my body was swinging towards the end of my practice. Today Sadhan was for 75 min, where I experienced getting into deep meditative and silent mode. Last night it was tough to get some sleep, as it was like voices and my thoughts were repeated in my head, and I could not stop them. I felt exhausted today because of a lack of sleep.

My response: First of all, very sorry to hear about the demise of your loving father. Our sympathy and prayers are with you. May his soul rest in peace. The kriyas that arise during the sadhan are nothing more than a manifestation of the clean-up process of your accumulated karmas. Your solid emotional thoughts create new karmas, and your kundalini energy is trying to clear your impressions. These impressions take lots of time to get removed as they are deeply rooted in Chitta. Slowly you will come out of your emotional state. Please continue your sadhan the same way.

Question: A practitioner: Yesterday, I did Sadhan for 1 hour and 50 minutes, and today, for the same duration. Today I went deeper. Yesterday I had a very "mental" kind of sadhan, many thoughts I couldn't get rid of - of my past love, someone that hurt me. I was very emotional today and felt like I was losing myself in those emotions. I have fallen down to my "egoistic ways" again. These thoughts were overbearing and overwhelming, but today's sadhan brought me back to the correct state. I am at ease again.

My response: Very nice. All past sensual impressions are getting cleared; that is why they manifest as memories during sadhan.

Question: A practitioner: Can I listen to mantra audio while I meditate? I am used to this kind of guided meditation.

My response: Avoid listening to audio during sadhan. Otherwise, it will merely be a guided meditation. We don't practice meditation. Maansik (mental) Japa is the best way to do sadhan. Just completely surrender to your Guru and recite your mantra mentally for maximum benefit.

Question: A practitioner: During sadhan, I feel energy rising to my throat and getting stuck like a balloon (blown) in a pipe. My facial expressions change, my eyes are shut, and I see a shining light.

My response: Please don't bother about it too much. It will rise to your cerebral region also later. You need to continue with your sadhan regularly. That is it. Many times, you may find only a specific Chakra active. The movement of kundalini energy along the cerebrospinal system is very disorderly and erratic. Therefore, please don't entertain any doubts.

Question: A practitioner: When do we decide to stop the sadhan? I mean during a session after sitting down.

My response: There is no specific rule on that. Depends upon your capability to sit, but one should not do sadhan by forcing oneself.

Question: A practitioner: Since yesterday's sadhan, I have been feeling so bored of me. I do not like to eat; if I eat also, I feel no taste. I do not want to talk. I don't feel like doing anything. Is it kriya or some illness? It started at two o'clock after sadhan. In the Morning, when I wake up, I feel happy, and after I have done sadhan, I feel lethargic. I feel heavy in my head. Please guide me.

My response: I understand that you are probably referring to yesterday's sadhan. Your mood swings are very normal. There is no need to do anything about it. After Shaktipat, everything is indeed a kriya, provided you are doing your sadhan regularly. Otherwise, this principle will not apply to you. Please remember this. I don't know whether you are doing your sadhan regularly or not. If it is, then your mood swings are kriyas. Otherwise, they could be anything else, including a disease.

Question: A practitioner: If we have a short time and there is a possibility of abrupt interruption, is there some way we can

Secrets of Shaktipat and Kundalini Yoga

still meditate? So, to sustain the meditative current generated in half an hour to the one-hour session, we meditated undisturbed.

My response: Actually, what you say does not apply to our path. It applies to meditation-based independent yoga systems like Ashtanga Yoga or Raja Yoga. There is no meditation in a real sense in our path. I mean, you don't focus your mind on anything once kriyas begin. You are only sitting in a meditative posture. But inside your mind, you are supposed to do nothing. Just sit and observe the reactions like a mute spectator. Whatever has to happen will happen involuntarily inside your body.

Therefore, where is the question of any meditation here? Please don't compare all the literature you read about meditation with our path. You can do your practice or remain in a state of witness as much time as possible. You can even remain in such a state throughout the day while simultaneously doing your daily work. I hope you got a general idea now.

Question: A practitioner: I have been doing my sadhan off and on. Sometimes I experience kriyas, but they are always the same on all occasions. I feel stretching of my neck either sideways or backward. Does this mean anything in particular?

My response: I am happy to know you are doing sadhan. Try and do it regularly so that you get benefitted from it faster. Otherwise, also you will get benefitted from whatever practice you are doing. But obviously, the progress will be slower.

Regarding your kriyas, please don't worry about them. They manifest as per your accumulated karmas which you are not aware of. The process of kriya manifestation will result in the neutralization of your accumulated karmas. Please don't worry if they are the same every time. In fact, you are not supposed to even look forward to experiencing a variety of kriyas. That will be against the principles of sadhan.

You are supposed to just surrender yourself completely to the divinity and continue with your practice regularly. That is the bottom line. Obviously, kriyas will go on over a prolonged period. If you practice regularly, the cosmic energy will ensure you don't get bored during meditation. It seems that is not happening due to your irregular sadhan.

Please understand this carefully. Sadhan should be continuous, even if it is periodical. It should be like a continuous flow of a river. That is how your karma will get washed at a rapid rate. Please don't worry about your personal life and future. Everything will unfold exactly the way it is supposed to happen. In the meantime, please focus your mind on the sadhan. Both journeys need to go parallel to each other.

The spiritual journey is dictating and controlling your materialistic life. Always focus on your Guru whenever possible and continue with your life. The more you invoke your Guru, the more you attract divine blessings.

Question: A practitioner: If I focus my eyes on a place in my body, I am experiencing some vibrations there. If I am focusing on the region, again and again, I am experiencing the vibrations again and again. If I start chanting the mantra in my mind and focus on my Guru Ji, the vibrations stop.

My response: That is a mistake people make. Once the kriyas start, you are not supposed to think of your Guru or your mantra. Just focus on the kriyas. Thinking of Guru will stop your kriya. Please keep this in mind.

Difference between meditation and sadhan

Question: A practitioner: How and when would I be able to do sadhan? I feel that if I am doing meditation, then sadhan will develop automatically. I guess so!

My response: You are getting confused. There is nothing known as meditation in our path. You only sit in meditation, but you don't do meditation. What you are supposed to do is

Secrets of Shaktipat and Kundalini Yoga

TO DO NOTHING when the kriyas start. For the kriyas to start, please focus your mind on your Guru and start chanting the mantra. Once kriyas begin, the mantra chanting will halt automatically, and you will not be able to focus on your Guru.

Therefore, please don't get confused between meditation and sadhan. Meditation is a totally different path. Otherwise, you will not make progress on any path. Just focus your mind only on your Guru, the mantra given to you, and nothing else. Otherwise, you will waste your time; the rest is up to you. I hope you have understood my above message. You are still getting confused. There is no need to think much about this. Just follow what was told to you and surrender entirely to God, Guru, or cosmic energy. That is the trick.

Using back support during sadhan

Question: A practitioner: Sharing my experiences during today's sadhan. It lasted for 4 hrs and 15 minutes. I experienced kriyas of bending, swinging, subtler rotations, and bigger jerks. Felt extremely cold. I had a couple of visions of massive light appearing in brightness. My back felt very restless. Can I use a pillow to support my back? Please guide.

My response: It is advisable not to take any support with a pillow because the spine will not be free and straight when you do sadhan with a pillow support. The simple thumb rule to be kept in mind is to keep the spine straight, preferably suspended freely. You can lie down on your bed and do sadhan also. But the same rule applies. The energy flow occurs along the spine while you are in sadhan. Especially in your case, you have been experiencing this energy flow intensely. Therefore, I suggest you, please avoid taking any support.

Question: A practitioner: When using an armchair for sadhan or lying down on the bed without a pillow, the back will be touching the chair/bed. Is that correct? Please explain the rules related to the sadhan position.

My response: Your spine needs to be straight and freely suspended if possible. That is the primary criterion here. Whether your back is touching something or not is not the primary criterion. However, preferably keep it freely suspended if you can. Otherwise, just ensure that it is kept straight. These rules apply to independent yoga systems like Ashtanga Yoga or Raja Yoga. However, since energy flow is involved here along the spinal system, keeping it straight and freely suspended as much as possible is better. Lastly, please remember that the awakened kundalini energy will automatically force you into the correct position. This happens, especially if you are regular in your sadhan. Therefore, please focus more on self-surrender.

Achieving milestones in sadhan

Question: A practitioner: Seeing lights, falling into spontaneous bliss, peace, etc., can these be seen as good karmas being worked out or eliminated? Or, should we rather see them as permanent milestones on our path that we crossed, indicative of the progress we have made in sadhan?

My response: Please don't focus on whether you have reached a particular benchmark in sadhan. That is against the principles of yoga practice. Instead, the mind should be focused purely on the sadhan itself. All kriyas are meant to clean up your karmas only. There is no doubt about this issue. Manifesting of kriya depends upon the karmas being cleaned at that point of time while you are in sadhan.

Predicting karma accumulated based on the kind of kriya being experienced is challenging. I don't have any supernatural powers to look into your past karmas. If you are experiencing bliss or peace, they can be related to karma being cleaned up. For example, you must have done lots of meditation in the past. Even those meditation sessions would have got accumulated as karma. They also need to be cleaned up, or it can be any other karma also. It could have been both good and bad.

Secrets of Shaktipat and Kundalini Yoga

Another example could be if a person was in the habit of taking intoxicants in their past lives. Those experiences also would have got accumulated. That is all we can say about it. It is not possible to predict them. You may have been in the habit of listening to some good music and experienced the peace of mind. Even such experiences must have got accumulated as karmas.

You can't interpret it as a milestone here because you need to be constantly experiencing the same state of mind, even when not in sadhan. But if your mind is focused in that direction, it will get tinged with egoism and become new karma. That is against the principle of Shaktipat sadhan also.

Please surrender entirely to the divinity and don't bother about the milestones, etc. A state of samadhi or thoughtlessness or bliss is totally a different thing. A lot of transformation of the mind takes place by then. You will come to know about it yourself. One of the indicators is the development of courage, dispassion, etc. Loss of idea of time lapsed during sadhan is another indicator. Seeing lights during sadhan is normal. They are called vishoka lights.

Distractions during sadhan

Question: A practitioner: Why does distraction happen on the path of spiritual quest, then leads to boredom. You blame the environment and the people around you. Seekers end up choosing distractions only to realize it was wrong. This creates anger, jealousy, competition, etc. How to surround yourself with experts/gnanis/motivators in life?

My response: When someone tries to fly to space away from planet earth, the gravitational force tries to pull down the spacecraft unless it reaches the escape velocity threshold. This happens because that's the way God has created humans and planet earth. That's the natural order of things. But we know that human effort makes it possible to leave planet earth. In ancient times, we also heard about great sages who traveled away from planet earth.

Similarly, Maya doesn't allow it to happen so easily when someone tries to free oneself from the eternal cycle of birth and death. However, it becomes easier if anyone exercises self-surrender to the Guru or God. Self-surrender to Guru or God is akin to reaching the escape velocity of a spacecraft. It all depends upon how much self-surrender is exercised by the sadhak. Suppose the self-surrender exercise approaches a specific benchmark. In that case, it becomes easy for the sadhak to free oneself from the binding power of Maya. Then there will no longer be any requirement of Guru either, just like the spacecraft doesn't need any booster rockets after reaching the escape velocity.

Distractions happen for sadhaks on the spiritual journey because they are manifested by Maya. However, the type of distractions manifested is in accordance with the kind of past accumulated karma. They are a means through which Maya tries to prevent the sadhak from escaping its binding power. Otherwise, how will it bind the sadhak within the realm of illusion?

A sadhak blaming the environment around or people for the problems is due to his egoism only. Otherwise, all life unfolding for the sadhak is self-created in the form of past accumulated karmas. It's just that a sadhak doesn't remember his past karmas and thinks he is a gem of a guy, whereas other people around him are stupid. He tries to blame people around him for all his problems. However, he doesn't give credit to other people when something good happens to him. At that stage, he bloats in the glory and attributes his success to his merit. This again occurs in turn due to his pride and egoism.

Hence, it's all part of Maya only, including boredom setting in during sadhan. However, nothing lasts forever. As karmas get burned down in larger and larger chunks, sadhak soon starts getting elevated to higher platforms.

Secrets of Shaktipat and Kundalini Yoga

The only way to hang on to the path of yoga without getting distracted by the world around is to engage the mind with yet another distraction known as Guru. That means a Guru acts as bait for the mind so that it doesn't stray from the path of yoga. Although in the end, Guru also needs to disappear for the sadhak. In a nutshell, a sadhak needs to use a thorn known as Guru to remove another thorn known as Maya or cosmic illusion. Both disappear in the end, leaving the sadhak alone but with absolute bliss. That's the secret of success in yoga.

Whatever has to happen needs to happen only through the medium of Guru tattva or God conceived as the idea of Guru. There is no other need to surround oneself with experts, gnanis (wise people), motivators, etc. They may end up further unsettling the mind of a sadhak. Although a truly wise man will only direct the sadhak back to his or her own Guru.

Lastly, the problem of human emotions like anger, jealousy, etc., are only temporary. As a sadhak starts burning down his or her karmas, they become immune to human emotions, including both positive and negative ones. Burning down the karma is the master technique. Everything else falls into its place after that. Therefore, sadhaks shouldn't focus on addressing worldly problems, including psychological issues, in isolation. Instead, they should focus on the core so that every problem gets addressed comprehensively. That core is called Guru.

On low motivation for doing sadhan

Question: A practitioner: For 2 to 3 days, I am not able to focus on sadhan. I don't even feel like doing sadhan. I don't want to do anything. Why am I feeling this way? Today morning I sat forcibly for about 1 hour. Guru Ji, I still feel materialistic, and lots of thoughts are coming. I am jealous of seeing others' experiences because they experience some enlightening and great things. I know that I am not supposed to be jealous. I know it is karma, but how can I control these thoughts?

My response: Please don't worry about it too much. It happens that way with everyone. It is normal. Please remember that yoga practice is a lifelong journey. A journey of self-realization! A journey into the unknown world! It takes time, obviously. Please have patience and perseverance. Please don't bother about the experiences of others. Everyone has a different stock of karma accumulated. Obviously, your experiences will be different. Just hang on to the path of yoga and be brave.

Miscellaneous issues

General doubts on spirituality

Question: A practitioner: My ego is tripping again, which demotivates me to do yoga. Hence the question. Most countries were under Anglo-Saxon regimes for centuries. India was the center of all kinds of education. In India, we had (have) many great yogis and Gurus. By people seeking spiritual paths during those days, did they cause slavery? How do we ensure success in all spheres through the spiritual path? Why does one choose one over the other?

My response: People seeking spiritual growth are a different subject altogether. It has been going on in India since ancient times, always eternally. Whereas geopolitics is another subject altogether. Hence, I have not understood your question correctly. However, only a few seek a spiritual path. As Krishna said in Gita, out of thousands of people, only one tries it. Only one reaches the ultimate goal of thousands of such people who try. However, all others who would have tried also reach some stage in their life and start once again in their next life. It's like sportsmen trying for Olympic gold.

Question: Same practitioner: Will kriya help us in the material world? Is it only for spiritual growth? What should one do to gain both?

Colonel T Sreenivasulu

Choosing only a spiritual path will impact not only the individual but also the family (generations) and perhaps the country's progress. Hence, I want to know if the downfall of India happened due to this rise in spiritual-seeking activities.

My response: Only karma will help you experience the material world in whichever way you want. But its outcome can't be predicted precisely.

On the other hand, kriya is akin to the process of evaporation of the camphor type of dirt. It is accumulated around the soul or spirit in the form of karma. Its impact is akin to the camphor fumes experienced by the person but physically, mentally, and intellectually.

The soul or spirit is none other than the core of the same human being. The same human being was earlier experiencing accumulated camphor kind of dirt, thinking that was only his existence. He couldn't realize earlier that he has all the power within him, only all the time. As the camphor dirt around him starts getting evaporated, he begins to realize, at last, his own infinite power. That's called spiritual growth.

Hence, kriyas destroy the material world of a person and make him cease to be a human being, thereby paving the way for his absolute power to manifest. However, the benefit of spiritual growth is for self only.

Just try to comprehend the implications intellectually. You will recollect all your past lives if you reach such a high level spiritually. The moment you realize that you had earlier incarnated innumerable times, you will simply laugh at yourself in your current life and quit your human body in a trice. You will no longer bother about your extensions in the form of your body, your family, your country, or anything else in the world.

However, one doesn't need to fear such a situation. The reason is it will happen in a very harmonious way. The all-knowing cosmic power will protect you. How it may impact your family or country materially can't be predicted precisely. Because your family and nation continue to remain within the realm of Maya while your self-realization has occurred.

However, your family and country would be blessed for having given birth to a spiritually awakened being like you. That's for sure. However, a sadhak need not be pessimistic, thinking about what good will accrue materially if his family is blessed. It's difficult to predict the ways of God. Divine grace operates in a mysterious way.

After Shaktipat initiation, a sadhak doesn't need to quit his profession or family and renounce worldly life as such. All that is being told to him is to exercise self-surrender and trust his Guru. Surely that won't cost him a penny. Then what's the hang-up?

How does it matter whether kriya helps him in the material world or not? He is, as such, engaged in doing his karma for survival.

Regarding the last part of the question, why the downfall of India happened is a matter of geopolitics. It has nothing to do with a few people pursuing spiritual growth. In any case, such people are always minuscule. Instead, most people would have actively pursued God but for all the wrong reasons.

In a nutshell, human beings never want God's grace. They want only the power of God, which is Maya in its pure form. Therefore, seeking God's grace truly means delivering them from the power of his Maya only; and not accumulating more of Maya.

Hence you can't desire to remain in a pool of mud on one side and clean yourself simultaneously. How can both phenomena be possible simultaneously? To clean up yourself, you must start stepping out of the mud pool first.

Question: A practitioner: There are uncountable past karmas stored in the subconscious mind. If kriyas burn all those karmas then, we can rise higher in the spiritual path?

Colonel T Sreenivasulu

Although you mentioned that kriya can start from any spot of the body, kindly tell me when the kriyas happening on physical aspects ends; then, it starts showing visuals like colorful light/specific shapes/creature/Guru images, etc.

After Shaktipat, all our Chakras are initiated; however, when do we realize its energy is fully activated? Like experiencing jerks, vibrations, etc., are observed; however, when do we know it is ready for the next level of Chakra activation?

At times, kriyas become aggressive, we heard. In what situation do we need Guru's intervention to control it? Have you ever been involved in such a situation?

Why does it get stored in memory when kriyas reveal our past lives? Does it not create new karma?

In Shaktipat deeksha, do we have a certain level of deekshas? When somebody attains a certain level need to have next-level deeksha?

You may ignore any of these questions if they seem not valid to be answered.

My response: I will answer your question in the same sequence paragraph-wise.

Para 1. Kriyas burn all past karmas. That is how you are spiritually elevated. Actually, you are the very divine spirit inside. Only the accumulated karma is removed like trash is cleaned from the mirror's surface.

Para 2. Kriyas manifest in a very disorderly manner. Hence, you can't predict when physical kriyas end and others begin.

Para 3. You have misunderstood this. Kriyas depend upon your past accumulated karmas. Jerks may not be experienced by everyone. Similarly, kundalini energy is fully activated after Shaktipat. You are trying to compare this with independent yoga systems like Ashtanga Yoga or Raja Yoga. In such yoga systems, kundalini energy is awakened step by step from Chakra to Chakra. But Shaktipat is a higher technique. That is why Shaktipat initiation is not given to everyone. It is given only to those who must have already undergone the preparatory stages in their past lives.

Para 4. There are a few sadhaks for whom kriyas have become aggressive. I make them stop doing sadhan temporarily and make them divert their minds.

Para 5. Some kriyas give an indication of past lives. If you emotionally attach to the kriyas, they become fresh karmas.

Para 6. Shaktipat deeksha is the same for everyone. There are no different levels.

I suggest you, please read my book on the compiled questions and answers. The book has answers to most of your above questions. Otherwise, it becomes difficult for me to answer each member individually, repeating my answers repeatedly. I will not be able to type elaborate answers also. Instead, you will get significantly benefitted if you read my book. Despite repeated requests, sadhaks are making the same mistake again and again. Kindly understand this. It becomes very easy for you and me if you read the books. If there is still anything you need clarification on, then you are most welcome to ask me questions. Otherwise, please read the book first.

Connecting with soul

Question: A practitioner: How to connect to our soul and how will our soul guide us?

My response: You and your soul are one and the same in principle. It is just that you think you are different. This thought arises due to your egoism. Therefore, once that egoism is disintegrated, you realize that you are that very soul or God with whom you wanted to connect. Therefore, there is nothing known as getting connected with anything; you alone are the only existence or truth or the very divinity. Obviously, nothing can guide you as such because you are supreme.

Colonel T Sreenivasulu

A Guru acts as a medium for you to make this return journey of self-realization. That is all about it. You are getting carried away by all the literary ideas, such as connecting with the soul or getting guidance from the soul, etc. Please understand that all such literature is mostly trash. It is more academic stuff. It is suitable only for writing books, giving lectures, and making money by confusing and fooling people. That kind of trash is not even classified as knowledge. Self-realization occurs only when you free yourself from all such trash. This process has begun for you after Shaktipat.

Therefore, please don't bother about all such academic stuff. They are basically linguistic gimmicks, a play of the words. Stupid questions are framed which have no rationale. In any case, the soul or God is supposed to be beyond rational reasoning. Therefore, how can such questions be framed in the first place? Please trust your Guru and seek the grace of God for your self-realization rather than getting distracted by the trash you mentioned above.

Sadhaks doubts form YouTube

Question: A practitioner: I accidentally stumbled upon a video on YouTube where a Guru is giving deeksha through a mantra, and I listened to the mantra. If, by any chance, I receive his energy, will there be any conflict?

My response: I have no idea regarding such things, please. How do they give deeksha through YouTube or whether it works or not? I can't comment on what you mentioned above. Whether you have received his energy or not is not certain. I can't confirm it. Please don't ask me to check out such videos, either. It will become too much of a workload for me. I hope you understand my problem. I am only a medium for Shaktipat deeksha.

However, please remember that anything you do will get accumulated as new karma. The more powerful the action, the more powerful the karma. In Shaktipat, a practitioner is trying to free themself from the karmas. Therefore, what you mentioned above has no connection with Shaktipat sadhan. It is akin to entering the mud simultaneously while trying to clean it. Does it make any sense? Further, it will slow down the progress.

Therefore, I suggest you, please don't do all such things mentioned above. You will be wasting your time and slowing down your progress on the path of yoga. However, if you get seriously interested in other yoga systems, then it is your wish. You need to decide in your mind firmly what you want and what your aim in life is.

Praying for worldly things

Question: A practitioner: Please forgive me if there is anything wrong in asking this. Can I pray to Amma (the cosmic power worshipped as the mother) for any particular desire?

My response: Yes, of course. It is your wish. But please remember that it will become a new karma. I mean, it is a different story if you are in some trouble. Otherwise, seeking materialistic benefits will become a new karma. It is akin to washing your feet and entering into the mud repeatedly. It is against the principle of yoga practice to seek the fulfillment of desires. That is the thumb rule to remember. Rest, it is up to you.

After death phenomenon

Question: A practitioner: I have a general question. You have given a glimpse of various possibilities of after-death scenarios. I would like to know what difference it makes in their after-death life between an uninitiated man and a man who had received Shaktipat.

My response: My knowledge about the after-death or after-life phenomenon is almost zero. It is a different subject altogether. It has nothing to do with yoga practice as such. However, technically speaking, there is no difference in the phenomenon experienced by ordinary people and those who have taken Shaktipat deeksha. However, people who have taken Shaktipat deeksha will surely meet another Shaktipat Guru in their next life unless they have stopped their sadhan before death. Otherwise, whatever little I have read on the subject, there is no other difference.

Question: A practitioner: What happens when we die? Are we going to exit as the animal? Or is there hell and paradise? Please let me know. People are doing a lot of good things, and also, a lot of people are killing animals and doing bad things.

My response: My knowledge of the after-life phenomenon is zero. That is a different subject. It really doesn't pertain to yoga practice. However, rebirth is a sure phenomenon after a person dies unless moksha is attained, in which case it is not classified as death. Only the physical body is discarded. In the case of people who don't attain moksha, they also simply discard their physical bodies, but transmigration takes place into new bodies. These new physical bodies could be either human or animal.

It is also possible that transmigration takes place into other dimensions or planes of existence, like hell, heaven, or others. But even such people need to be reborn again on the earthly plane later to attain their moksha or salvation. People who do good things will be rewarded for their actions accordingly, either in the same lifetime or after that. The same thing happens with people doing bad things.

Lastly, transmigration into other planes of existence, like hell or heaven, or simply into an animal or human body also depends upon the accumulated cumulative karma. It all depends upon the intensity of accumulated karma. If the power of good karmas is too great, the person will likely be born in heaven or other celestial planes. Similarly, if the intensity is not that great, they may be born as humans only but rewarded with all good things. The same phenomenon may occur in the opposite direction also. If the intensity of bad karma is too great, the person may undergo hell or other nether planes of existence.

If the intensity is less, he may be born a human and punished accordingly. But being born in animal wombs involves other issues like spiritual degeneration. It will not be merely a punishment; instead, it involves spiritual decline, although temporarily only. After being born in animal wombs once or a few times, again, the human body is recovered.

You need to understand the entire phenomenon comprehensively and not with isolated questions on the subject. Because while comprehending this, you also need to remember that everything, including earthly life or hell or heaven or anything else, is simply psychedelic. It is merely part of the overall cosmic illusion or Maya.

Necessity of clearing karma

Question: A practitioner: Why are we trying to clear karmas? I heard we are made of karma, and most karma is not bad? This could be a stupid question, but I am confused.

My response: As a human, what you think you are right now or what you undergo right now is due to the cumulative impact of your accumulated karma in your subconscious mind. But that doesn't mean that you are made of those karmas. You are only reeling under the impact of those karmas and thereby attributing everything to those karmas. Underneath this layer of karma, you are a different entity called God, etc.

As per your understanding, certain karmas are good, and certain karmas are bad. But please remember that it is strictly your personal opinion. What you think is good karma may not hold good under all conditions. It is very relative from situation to situation and from person to person. Unnecessarily we will enter into philosophical discussions, and it is not possible for me to explain it on this forum.

Please reread my book for insight into this. Do you visualize or think about this when your mind is in deep sleep or dream? All these questions arise only when you are in the waking state. Similarly, when you enter a state of thoughtlessness, all these doubts and dilemmas start to melt away.

This terminal state of mind is possible only by neutralizing your karmas. Therefore, please focus on attaining this terminal state of mind for the time being. Just still your mind, and you will start knowing everything. This is the teaching of all ancient yoga texts and most religions.

Praying to Guru

Question: A practitioner: Does the language of prayer make a difference? As a Guru may not be aware of that type of language of prayer, how will his or her prayers be answered?

My response: The language of prayer doesn't matter to the Guru or the student. The reason is that the prayer is not addressed to the Guru as a person. It is addressed to the Guru tattva or the essence of the Guru. That Guru tattva, or the essence of the Guru, is nothing but God only. It applies to the student and his Guru because a Guru is also invoking his own Guru. Thus, creating a kind of blockchain effect on God himself, who happens to be the first Guru for mankind.

Guidelines for women

Question: A practitioner: Can a woman in her monthly period practice sadhan regularly?

My response: Yes. No problem. There are no restrictions on the practitioner after three days of initiation. In fact, you can do it 24*7 irrespective of the condition. The only restriction is to avoid a public place and a place in public where the footfall or people are coming and going and watching you. Avoid these places. Otherwise, no restrictions, please.

Secrets of Shaktipat and Kundalini Yoga

Question: A practitioner: I had my baby recently, and you told me to wait for two weeks before starting my practice again. Caring for my baby and finding a quiet, peaceful time to meditate has been a challenge. Is it okay if I listen to my mantra via audio?

My response: Please wait till you complete two weeks period. After that, you can start doing sadhan again slowly. Till that time, please take a complete break. You don't even listen to the mantra till two weeks are over because listening to the mantra is also considered as sadhan only. It is not advisable for you after childbirth. Please don't worry about it. Just relax completely and take care of your new baby.

Question: Another practitioner: Why is a two weeks gap after childbirth necessary?

My response: She is one of the serious practitioners experiencing kriyas aggressively. When she asked me this question as to whether she could continue with the practice, I checked it out with my Guru ji, His Holiness. As per His Holiness, a lady's body will not be conducive enough in the immediate aftermath of childbirth. Hence, the reason for giving a gap of two weeks! I request all the affected sadhaks to please make a note of this. This is a crucial direction from His Holiness. I may forget it; that is why I want to place it on record.

Glossary

Aham: Egoism or the principle of "I" in a human being!
Ajna chakra: The energy center between the two eyebrows in a human body.
Akash tatva: It means the essence of the element ether. As per the ancient Sanskrit texts, the cosmos comprises five elements, including the human body. They are earth, water, fire, air, and ether. However, modern science doesn't yet recognize the existence of the fifth element, 'ether.'
Anahata chakra: The energy center located at the heart region of the spine.
Anahata sound: The sound produced without anything being struck and could be heard by someone internally.
Asana: It is a yogic posture. Yoga practitioners practice various asanas in preparation for meditation-based Ashtanga yoga.
Apan: The life force that operates in the body's lower region!
Ashram: The yogic retreat. It is the residence of a Guru or the venerable teacher under whom people practice yoga.
Ashtanga yoga: This is also called Raja Yoga. It is a meditation-based yoga system. It has eight preparatory levels or stages.
Ashtami: The eighth day after the full moon or new moon as per the lunar calendar system in India!

Secrets of Shaktipat and Kundalini Yoga

Ashtami havan: A sacrificial fire ceremony performed on the eighth day during the Navaratri or the nine-day festive season in India in honor of the supreme cosmic power.

Anavee deeksha: An initiation into practicing any yoga system or other method aimed at materialistic fulfillment before awakening kundalini energy in a person.

Anuvopay: The technique used for giving anavee deeksha!

Bhagavad Gita: The literal meaning is the song celestial. It is a sacred Sanskrit text of the Hindus. It is in the form of teaching by Lord Krishna to his friend and the Pandava prince, Arjun. He refused to fight the battle to avoid killing his relatives on the opposing side. This text is part of the famous epic Mahabharat of the Hindus.

Bhakti yoga: A yoga system based on a person's devotion to a particular God or Goddess. Here, faith is used to achieve the stillness of the mind. Usually, this kind of yoga practice is suitable for temperamental persons by nature.

Brahman: The supreme divinity pervading all cosmos and beyond, God or Almighty, etc.!

Brahmacharya: The practice of celibacy!

Brahma muhurta: This begins approximately one hour and thirty minutes before sunrise! It is considered the most auspicious time for any work and yoga practice.

Buddhi: It is a form of the cosmic energy called the 'intellect' in a person or the discriminating faculty, along with which egoism is co-located.

Chakra: An energy center in the cerebrospinal system!

Chamunda: One of the Indian goddesses worshipped in the city of Dewas in India.

Chidakash: The mind space!

Darshan: The opportunity to see a person or any other thing!

Deeksha: The formal procedure of giving initiation into a yoga system to a practitioner by their Guru. It is usually done at an auspicious time on an auspicious day selected for the purpose.

Deekshadhikara: The formal authorization to give deeksha to any person by a spiritual or yoga Guru to one of their disciples. After this authorization, the disciple formally becomes a spiritual or yoga Guru. This authorization can be given to more than one disciple also.
Dhanteras puja: A worship ceremony performed at the Dhanteras festival in India.
Dholak: A kind of musical instrument of India!
Dhyan Mudra: The meditative posture and gesture!
Guru: The venerable teacher who drives away the darkness of ignorance from a student's mind so that the light of knowledge already inside the Self shines forth!
Guru Gita: The song celestial in adoration of Guru. It is part of an ancient Sanskrit text called Markandeya Purana. It teaches the essence of the Guru and how to worship him as God or the Almighty. It is available as a separate book on many publishing platforms.
Gunas: The three qualities of the mind-stuff.
Japa: Repetition of mantra!
Ji: It is a suffix added at the end of any name or a professional as a mark of respect in the Hindi language in India. The same suffix might be in use in more Indian languages as well.
Jnana yoga: This is a system based on the path of knowledge. Usually, this kind of yoga practice is suitable for intellectual-type people.
Kaali: The Goddess of destruction or the primordial supreme cosmic power in the destructive form!
Kailash parvat: Kailash Mountain in the Himalayan ranges!
Kamakhya Devi: A Goddess worshipped at Guwahati city in the Assam state of India.
Kalighat: A Goddess worshipped at Kalighat in India.
Kanyakumari: A Goddess of India worshipped in the city of Kanyakumari in the Tamil Nādu state of India. It is located at the southernmost tip of India.
Kartal: A kind of musical instrument of India.
Kathak: A kind of dance form of India!

Secrets of Shaktipat and Kundalini Yoga

Kawali: A kind of dance gesture of India!

Kriya: The involuntary reaction in body, mind, and external daily life that manifests to clean a person's mind of all its sensual impressions!

Kundalini: The supreme primordial cosmic energy that manifests in the universe's form. This energy is located at the base of the cerebrospinal system in every human being, halfway between the anus and the genital region.

Lakshmi: Goddess of sustenance or the primordial supreme cosmic power in sustaining forms!

Lingam: The phallus! Followers of Lord Shiva worship him in the form of a phallus.

Ma Durga: The Goddess Mother Durga worshipped in India.

Mahalakshmi: The Great Goddess of sustenance or the primordial supreme cosmic power in sustaining forms!

Mala: A string of Rudraksha beads used for counting while repeating a mantra.

Maya: Cosmic illusion or cosmic energy in its most basic form!

Manipura: The energy center located in the navel region of the spine.

Manjunatha: Lord Shiva!

Mantra: It is a sacred Sanskrit syllable, a word, a sentence, or a group of sentences that could run into any amount of text.

Mantra Shastra: The science dealing with the mantras! So many ancient texts are available in Sanskrit dealing with this subject.

Mazira: A kind of musical instrument of India!

Meenakshi: A Goddess of India worshipped in the city of Madurai in the Tamil Nādu state of India.

Moksha: Moksha means salvation or freedom from the cycle of life and death for any creature. As per the ancient Sanskrit texts, this is possible only for humans. Moksha is not feasible for other creatures, including celestial beings and demons.

Mudra: A special yoga gesture!

Mookambika: A Goddess worshipped in India.

Muladhara chakra: The energy center located at the base of the cerebrospinal system, halfway between the anus and the genital region.

Naada: The primordial vibration that caused the beginning of the cosmos!

Nadis: Subtle channels of energy!

Nadi shuddhi: It means cleaning the subtle channels of energy. Nadi shudhi is usually done by practicing pranayama. It is a yoga technique.

Nadi sodhana: Pumping out the impurities from the subtle energy channels!

Naga baba: The mendicants who roam around yielding a trident. They are usually followers of Lord Shiva. They are usually found wandering around without wearing clothes, and their bodies are smeared with ashes.

Navratri: It means nine nights. However, these nine days are a festive season for Hindus in India. Usually, many serious devotees observe fasting during this period. This period is for worshipping the supreme cosmic power or the divine as Mother Goddess as per the tradition of Shaktas or energy worshippers.

Ojas: When people practice celibacy, sex energy converts into this substance. It is supposed to be climbing up the Sushumna Nadi or the central channel of the spine. As a result, it gives people a powerful aura to attract the masses. Wherever a person is seen in society displaying extraordinary genius and impacting a large population, it is due to the power of these substances!

Padmasana: The lotus posture of the asana!

Parampara: The lineage or the order of monks of any tradition or yoga system!

Parashakthi: The supreme primordial cosmic energy!

Parayanam: Recitation!

Patanjali Yoga Sutras: An ancient Sanskrit treatise on Ashtanga or Raja yoga. This text is considered the most authoritative text on the meditation-based yoga system.

Secrets of Shaktipat and Kundalini Yoga

Pran: Pran is a form of cosmic or kinetic energy pervading the entire cosmos. It is also the life force pervading the 'sheath of life force' in a human body.

Pranam: It simply means salutations. People in India use this word while greeting elders or venerable persons in society, usually accompanied by both palms, standing or kneeling. Sometimes prostration of the body is also done on the ground.

Pran Vayu: It is the life force in the form of an invisible gas that operates in the upper region of the human body.

Pranayama: It is a part of Ashtanga or Raja yoga. It deals with the science of breathing to achieve control over the life force that exists within the human body.

Puja: Worshipping ceremony in India!

Rajas: One of the three qualities of the mind due to which creativity manifests in all forms.

Raja yoga: This is also called Ashtanga yoga. It is a meditation-based yoga system. It has eight preparatory levels or stages.

Ramayan: It is an ancient Sanskrit text of India. It is an epic that describes the deeds of Prince Rama, who is worshipped as a divine incarnation of God in India. The prince was born in an ancient kingdom of the Indian subcontinent and later became its ruler.

Rishis: Sages of India!

Sadhana: It is the voluntary practice done by a person tinged with human egoism before kundalini energy has been awakened in their body.

Sadhan: It is the phenomenon of involuntary practice inside the human body, mind, and external daily life after kundalini energy has awakened.

Sadhak: A practitioner of any yoga or tantric system!

Sahasrara: The energy center located at the crown of the head.

Samsara: The worldly existence or life experienced by a human or any other creature. According to ancient texts, it is presumed to be only psychedelic.

Samadhi: It is a state of thoughtlessness. It is the terminal objective of all yoga practices before self-realization can occur!
Sankalpa: It is free will exercised by humans in their minds!
Sakshi bhavam: The state of a mute witness or mindfulness in a human being! It is a term applied to the human psyche.
Saraswati: The Goddess of creation or the primordial supreme cosmic power in the creative form!
Satvic: One of the three qualities of the mind due to which the function of maintenance or sustenance manifests in all forms.
Shastra: The word means science. However, it is usually used when reference is made to the ancient Sanskrit texts on various sciences.
Shakthopay: The technique used for giving Shaktipat deeksha or initiation. Here, cosmic energy, or the Shakthi, is used as the tool.
Shambhavi deeksha: Shambhavi deeksha or initiation is a state reached by a person. There's no more initiation or deeksha at this state as such, although often misunderstood by people. This state should be reached at the end of yoga practice using Shakthopay.
Shambhavopay: The alleged technique used for giving Shambhavi deeksha or initiation.
Shambhavi mudra: The yoga gesture allegedly used by people to give shambhavi deeksha!
Shanthi: Absolute peace!
Shakthas: The energy worshippers in India! They worship God in the form of cosmic energy.
Shaktipat: 'The descent of energy' It is a technique the Order of Shaktipat monks uses to initiate a practitioner into the Siddha Mahayoga system.
Shakti: The primordial cosmic energy!
Shakti Peeta: The primordial cosmic energy center!
Shiva murti: Form of Lord Shiva!
Shri Phal: Coconut!

Secrets of Shaktipat and Kundalini Yoga

Siddha Mahayoga: The grand yoga system encompassing all the individual yoga systems after the kundalini energy is woken up in a person. It is the yoga system practiced by 'The Order of Shaktipat.'
Surya tratak: A tantric practice involving focusing of concentration on the Sun.
Sushumna: The central channel of the spine in the human body!
Sushumna Nadi: The subtle channel of energy in the human body's central canal of the spine!
Svadhisthana chakra: The energy center is located near the root of the genital region in the cerebrospinal system.
Tamas: One of the three qualities of the mind due to which destruction manifests in all forms.
Tandhra: As per yoga texts, it is a state between the dream state and the waking state.
Tantra: A form of the yoga system.
Tantric: Practitioner of tantra! A form of yoga system!
Tattva: The essence of a thing!
Trishul: The trident wielded by Lord Shiva!
Vaastu: The ancient Indian science about ideal architectural aspects.
Vairagya: It is a state of mind when interest is lost in both the external and internal worlds, which are materialistic.
Vaishnodevi: The Goddess is located in the Trikuta Mountains in the Himalayas in the State of Jammu and Kashmir in India. It is the most popularly worshipped energy center.
Vedanta: It is one of the six systems of Indian philosophies.
Virat Kali: The Goddess of destruction in her complete universal form.
Vishuddha: The energy center is located in the throat region of the spine!
Yogi: The practitioner of any yoga system!
Yogini: The lady practitioner of any yoga system!
Yam: The seed mantra sound of the heart chakra or the Anahata chakra.

Ashrams of the Shaktipāt Order
(Traceable & Autonomous)

1. Yogeshwari Rachna, Tarkeswar Siddha Mahayoga Foundation, Bhira Kheri, Lakhimpur Kheri, Uttar Pradesh, PIN – 262901, India, Mobile: +91 945 022 0221, Email: tsfoundation21@gmail.com

2. Siddha Yogini Thanishka, Melbourne Beach, Florida, USA, Mobile: +1(321)960-0445, Email: supriyavarmakurup@gmail.com

3. Goddess Vartika Shukla, Siddha Mahayoga Foundation, 806, New Anand Apartment, Plot 47, Sector 56, Gurugram, Haryana, PIN-122011, India, Mobile: +91-9819962635, Email: vartikashukla2000@gmail.com

4. Sadguru Hagi, Melbourne, Victoria, Australia, +61 407 683 465, Email: ghracer@hotmail.com

5. Yogi Virendra, Ghaziabad, Uttar Pradesh, India, +91-9999290388, Email: virendrasfarswan@gmail.com

6. Yogi Abhishek Vashist, Jaipur, Rajasthan, India, +91

Secrets of Shaktipat and Kundalini Yoga

9079121514, Email: abhijagriya@gmail.com

7. Yogi Gautam, Hyderabad, Telangana, India, +91 9963359922, Email: yogi.shaktipat@gmail.com

8. Mahayogini Ramya Devi, Bengaluru, Karnataka, India, Mobile: +91 988 023 9480, Email: yoginiramyadevi25@gmail.com

9. Yogi Puneet Parashar, Dubai, UAE, Mobile: +971 52 867 6684, Email: puneetparashar39@gmail.com

10. Mahayogini Manisha, New Delhi, India, Mobile: +91 799 110 9595, Email: mabmanisha@gmail.com

11. Yogini Vijaya, Johannesburg, South Africa, Mobile: +27 83 682 2286, Email: juss@mplanet.co.za

12. Yogeshwari Parameshwari, Jangaon, Telangana, India, Mobile: +91 9704424072, Email: sreenivasashaktipatfoundation@gmail.com

13. Yogi Shalin Kumar, Kollam, Kerala, India, Mobile: +91-8281219592, Email: shalin_kumar@sahajananda-ashram.com

14. Yogi Ramganapathy, East Godavari, Andhra Pradesh, India, Mobile: +91 9494546139, Email: ramaganapathi@sahajananda-ashram.com

15. Yogini Shikha, Gurugram, Haryana, India, Mobile: +91-9560046782, Email: shikhatiwari512@gmail.com

16. Yogi Shyam Gwalani, Nashik, Maharashtra, India, Mobile: +91-8275798148, Email: shyampgwalani@gmail.com

17. Yogini Aatmika, Chennai, Tamil Nadu, India, Mobile:

Colonel T Sreenivasulu

+91 9080570782, Email: aathmika61@gmail.com

18. Yogini Sreedevi, Hyderabad, Telangana, India, Mobile: +91 9849590088, Email: siri0404@gmail.com

19. Yogi Bharadwaja, Richmond, Virginia, USA, Mobile: +1 (973) 393-4135, Email: bradyogapath@gmail.com

20. Yogini Mahalakshmi, Visakhapatnam, Andhra Pradesh, India, Mobile: +91 8008596898, Email: laxmi674@gmail.com

21. Yogini Sumitra Devi, Rajahmundry, Andhra Pradesh, India, Mobile: +91 8309180149, Email: sumitraprasad45@gmail.com

22. Yogini Ramadan, Lincoln, Nebraska, USA, Mobile: +1(402)217-2363, Email: ramadanwesal@gmail.com

23. Yogi Ranjeet, Pune, India, Mobile: +91 8899992493, Email: ranjeetakolkar@gmail.com

24. Yogi Ranga, Hyderabad, India, Mobile: +91 9866305772, Email: rangathrive@gmail.com

25. Yogi Akhilesh, Gaziabad, UP, India, Mobile: +91 8586925095, Email: yogiakhilesh4622@gmail.com

26. Yogi Heyrman, Zandhoven, Belgium, +32 488137186, Email: andrehey@yahoo.com

27. Yogi Gnaneswar, Hongkong, China, Mobile: +852 91931419, Email: ggnan.g@gmail.com

28. Yogini Joanna, Vienna, Austria, Mobile: +43 681 10226745, Email: joanna@scenicdesign.org

Secrets of Shaktipat and Kundalini Yoga

29. Mr. Ravi Kumar Kousik, Hyderabad, India, Mobile: +91 8978611137

30. Mr. Ajay Humsagar, Hyderabad, India, Mobile: +91 9449824331

31. Mr. Nageswar Rao, Andhra Pradesh, India, Mobile: +91 8639139422

32. Mr. Kamalesh Padiya, Pune, Maharashtra, +91 9765800457, +91 8530390457

33. Narayan Kuti Sanyas Ashram, Tekri Road, Devas, Madhya Pradesh, India, PIN – 455001, Tele: +91 0727223891/31880, Mobile: +91 9977968108

34. Swami Vishnu Tirth Sādhan Seva Nyas, 12-3, Old Palasiya, Jopat Koti, Indore, Madhya Pradesh, India, PIN – 452001, Tel: +91 0731 566386/564081, Mobile: +91 9713468347

35. Swami Shivom Tirth Kundalini Yoga Center, Durga Mandir, Near Collector Bungalow, Chindwada, Madhya Pradesh, India, PIN – 480001, Tel: +91 07162 42640

36. Swami Shivom Tirth Ashram, Mukarji Nagar, Raisan, Madhya Pradesh, India, PIN – 464551, Tele: +91 07482 22294

37. Swami Shivom Tirth Maha Yog Ashram, Khari Ghat, Jabalpur, Madhya Pradesh, India, PIN – 482008, Tel: +91 0761 665027

38. Devatma Shakthi Society,74, Navali Village, Post Dhahisar (via Mumbra), Mumbra Panvel Road, Thane

Colonel T Sreenivasulu

District, Maharashtra, India, PIN – 400612, Tel: +91 022 7411400

39. Shivom Kripa Ashram Trust, House No. 28-1463/1, Tene Banda, Shivom Nagar, Chittor, Andhra Pradesh, India, PIN – 517004, Tel: +91 9440069096, 08572 49048

40. Yog Shree Peeth Ashram, Shivanand Nagar, Muni- kirethi, Rishikêsh, Uttarakhand, India, PIN – 249201, Tel: +91 0135 430467

41. Om Kar Ashram, Veraval, Gujarat, India

42. Om Kar Sādhan Ashram, Anand, Gujarat, India

43. Swami Vishnu Tirth Gnana Sadhan Ashram, Kubudu Road, Kedi Gujjar, Gannur, Sonepat District, Haryana, India, Tel: +91 0124 62150/61550

44. Vishnu Tirth Sidha Mahayog Samstanam, Shivom Kuti Ashram, Near Kaleshwar Mandir, Bhahadurpur Road, Amalner Post, Jalgaon District, Maharashtra, India, PIN – 425401

45. Guru Niketan, Shiva Colony, Dabra, Gwalior Dist, Madhya Pradesh, PIN – 475110, Tel: +91 07524 22153

46. Swami Shivom Tirth Ashram, Route No. 97, Pond Eddy, Sulivan Country, New York, U.S.A

47. Swami Maheshwaranand Tirtha, Sunwaha, Raison District, Madhya Pradesh, India, +91 7697648720

Monks of the **Shakthipāth** Order (Traceable History)

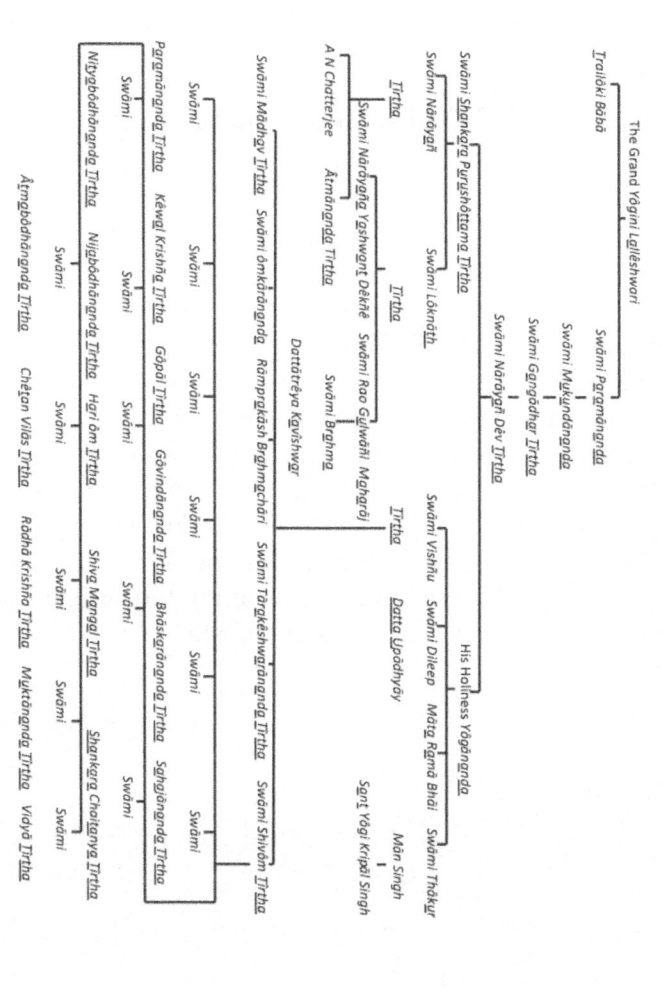

- The Grand Yōginī Lallēshwarī
  - Trailōki Bābā
    - Swāmi Paramānanda
      - Swāmi Mukundānanda
        - Swāmi Gangādhar Tīrtha
          - Swāmi Nārāyaṇ Dēv Tīrtha
            - His Holiness Yōgānanda
              - Swāmi Vishñu Tīrtha
                - Datta Upādhyāy
                  - Sgt. Yōgi Kripal Singh
              - Swāmi Dileep Tīrtha
              - Māta Ramā Bhāi
                - Mān Singh
              - Swāmi Thākur
            - Swāmi Shankara Puryshōttama Tīrtha
              - Swāmi Nārāyañ
                - Swāmi Lōknāth
                  - Swāmi ōmkārānanda
                    - Swāmi Brahma
                    - Dattātrēya Kaẏishwar
                  - Rāmprakāsh Brahmachāri
                  - Swāmi Targkēshwarānanda Tīrtha
                    - Swāmi Shivām Tīrtha
                      - Sahajānanda Tīrtha
                        - Swāmi
                          - Swāmi
                            - Vidyā Tīrtha
                      - Shankara Chaitanya Tīrtha
                        - Swāmi
                          - Swāmi
                            - Muktānanda Tīrtha
                    - Shiva Mangal Tīrtha
                      - Swāmi
                        - Swāmi
                          - Rādhā Krishṇa Tīrtha
                    - Bhāskarānanda Tīrtha
                      - Swāmi
                        - Swāmi
                          - Chētan Vilās Tīrtha
                    - Govindānanda Tīrtha
                      - Swāmi
                        - Swāmi
                          - Ātmabōdhānanda Tīrtha
                  - Swāmi Mādhav Tīrtha
                - Swāmi Nārāyaṇ Yashwant Dēkhē
                  - Ātmānanda Tīrtha
                  - Swāmi Rao Gujwāri Mahārāj
            - A N Chatterjee
            - Paramānanda Tīrtha
              - Kēwal Krishṇa Tīrtha
                - Gōpāl Tīrtha
                  - Hari ōm Tīrtha
                    - Nijabōdhānanda Tīrtha
                      - Swāmi
                        - Nityabōdhānanda Tīrtha

About the author

The author is an alumnus of some of the prestigious institutions of India, like Sainik School Korukonda, the National Defense Academy, and the Indian Military Academy. At the age of fifteen, he was attracted to the mighty Himalayan ranges and the source of the river Ganga due to his passion for rock climbing and mountaineering. His long journey of more than two thousand kilometers led to a different trip after encountering his Himalayan master on board the same train as a young boy! Unknown to the young lad, God had already scripted his journey long before it began! The author presently serves in the Indian Army and is a Great Grand Guru in the lineage of Shaktipat.

Made in United States
Orlando, FL
05 February 2024